# SAVING THE GIANT

# PANDA

# SAVING THE GIANT
# PANDA

# TERRY L. MAPLE, PH.D.

Professor of Psychology
Elizabeth Smithgall Watts Professor of Conservation & Behavior, Georgia Institute of Technology

President & Chief Executive Officer, Zoo Atlanta

LONGSTREET PRESS
Atlanta

Published by
LONGSTREET PRESS
2140 Newmarket Parkway
Suite 122
Marietta, GA 30067

Printed in the United States of America

1st printing 2000

Library of Congress Catalog Card Number: 00-105140

ISBN: 1-56352-615-8

Cover photograph by Joe Sebo for Zoo Atlanta

Jacket and book design by Burtch Bennett Hunter

This book is dedicated with affection and respect
to my brothers, M. Brian Maple and Max Oliver Maple,
and to the memory of our beloved parents.

# ~ CONTENTS ~

FOREWORD: BY ANDREW YOUNG
XI

AUTHOR'S PREFACE
XIII

I. WHO ARE THESE PANDAS, ANYWAY?
1

II. PANDAS AND PEOPLE
15

III. PANDIPLOMACY
27

IV. PANDAMONIUM
43

V. OBSERVING PANDAS
55

VI. CARING FOR PANDAS
69

VII. BECOMING WORTHY OF PANDAS
85

VIII. TALKING ABOUT PANDAS
1o1

IX. SAVING THE GIANT PANDA
115

EPILOGUE: THE EXTENDED PANDA FAMILY
129

REFERENCES
135

# SAVING THE GIANT
# PANDA

# – FOREWORD –

BY ANDREW YOUNG

Perhaps the oldest desire of humankind is to be able to live in harmony with its family, neighbors, and the environment. Yet peace is not automatic. From the beginning of time, peace had to be negotiated and protected in order for us to survive as a species. Peace is the result of wise and creative negotiation with those forces and persons with whom interaction is necessary for survival.

Abiding peace is a result of creative interactions that grow out of understanding our differences and learning to appreciate them as contributors to the pool of human experience. It is derived from trust, the knowledge that we are mutually dependent on each other for survival.

But for peace to prevail, we must work to overcome fear. Fear is our initial response to the unknown. It prepares us for fight or flight. Fear is replaced by enlightenment and understanding as we learn of our mutual needs to sustain life through compassion, security, and peace.

Over the years, our interest in giant pandas has urged us from paths of fear to cautious optimism, hope, and understanding. The systematic and sensitive search for survival of the lovable creature is described passionately by Terry Maple in this beautiful book. The relationship between America's zoos and the scientists of China is one of the many threads that are helping us to bridge the historic gap between the United States and China.

First, it has sown an American citizen who is primarily concerned with preserving a precious resource for China and the world. It has revealed a warm and humanitarian segment of American civilization and culture not seen in most of our commercial and diplomatic encounters.

Second, it has helped both sides to see the "intricate web of mutuality" that is necessary for human, panda, and environmental survival.

Third, the lovable panda has won the hearts of people of all ages and helped us to be more sensitive to the fragility of our own survival and the preservation of both human and animal habitat.

The Prophet Isaiah speaks of a glorious vision of the "lion and the lamb" lying down together and none shall be afraid. As we see the progress we are making in the coexistence of bamboo jungles and billions of Chinese citizens, we also see pandas reminding us of our common humanity. It is not too great a stretch to envision our mutual survival in peace and prosperity. In a strange and wonderful way, our love for the giant panda is leading us slowly to a deeper understanding of China. Our delicate contact on behalf of this wondrous creature is forcing us to overcome our fear.

My personal introduction to giant pandas began when I met the male An An while visiting the London Zoo in September 1978. As a card-carrying animal behaviorist, I was entitled to a behind-the-scenes moment including the opportunity to feed the awesome critter. Thinking of pandas as benign and lovable animals, I was stunned when he suddenly and violently lunged for the bamboo in my hand, nearly grabbing me by the throat in the process! Yes, I thought at the time, this beast is a bear, after all.

In 1984, while a fledgling zoo director, it became clear to me that giant pandas had a special power to attract people and to generate powerful emotional responses. Many zoos were then "renting" pandas for brief periods, and people by the hundreds of thousands were captivated as they flocked to zoos with the resources to exhibit pandas: Los Angeles, San Francisco, San Diego, Cincinnati, Memphis, Tampa, New York, Toledo, Columbus (Ohio). Then, as now, the "rent" for a pair of pandas was $100,000 per month, a very expensive exhibition, indeed. Although Atlanta's zoo was still in crisis in 1984, I was confident that we would someday be equal to the challenge of exhibiting giant pandas. But my dream was even more complicated. My scientific self longed for the opportunity to study this charismatic creature.

In a career eyeblink, now sixteen years since our first serious inquiry, the giant pandas have arrived in Atlanta. It has been worth the wait, and this book is my way of sharing the travails, the intrigue, and the emotional roller coaster that have been such integral parts of this arduous and complex journey. In the process of telling our story, I have addressed some larger, more mysterious issues: Just what is it about the giant panda species that generates such fawning and fussing? And why are zoo directors willing to move heaven and earth to acquire them? More important, surely, why have these animals been so difficult to reproduce in China and elsewhere throughout their lengthy history in captivity?

My personal quest to know pandas has been the most complex and challenging engagement of my zoo career. Like the task of rebuilding the zoo itself, it has tapped every talent and tested every deficiency in the fabric of my personhood. I was first trained as a behavioral scientist, and it was Zoo Atlanta's strength in science that enabled the zoo to qualify as a center for research on giant panda biology and behavior. But the going was rough throughout the ordeal of gaining approval from a diversity of idiosyncratic agencies, entities, and individuals. In college I once prepared for a career in the Foreign Service, and it was surely diplomacy that finally brought the giant pandas to Atlanta. (Little did I know in 1964 that I would someday carry a portfolio for the world's wildlife, a nation badly in need of effective representation.)

In charting this diplomatic path, I was advised by some of Atlanta's most esteemed statesmen. My greatest debt is to President Jimmy Carter, who supported and encouraged me for fifteen long years. His contacts at the highest levels of the Chinese government were invaluable, and his insight never failed to illuminate the correct path to a decision or a plan. In the final moments, I was uplifted by the efforts and encouragement of Senator Max Cleland and of Congressman John Lewis. Mr. Cleland's contacts in Beijing saved the project in the eleventh hour. Over the course of more than a decade, I also received local support from Georgia governors Joe Frank Harris, Zell Miller, and Roy Barnes, who grasped in sequence the vision of giant panda conservation. I especially appreciate the insight of Lt. Governor Mark

Taylor, who taught me that pandas could energize public education and motivate Georgia's school-age children. Finally, I thank former Speaker of the House Newt Gingrich, who made me understand the enormity of this opportunity, and never let me back down.

Our project has been sustained by private fundraising. For their leadership at a critical time I thank Doug Ivester and Donald Green of The Coca-Cola Company, and Gary Lee and Everne Cooper of United Parcel Service. Their early enthusiasm ensured that our panda campaign would be successful in the corporate community. For advice on planning the campaign, I thank my good friend Martin Gatins. The "Save a Species" campaign continues in Phase II under the careful management of Greg Harris.

For their friendship, patience, and understanding for so many years, I am truly grateful to an entire population of Chinese friends and colleagues. Among them, Dr. Zhang Anju has been a tireless advocate for the Atlanta-Chengdu partnership, and I have greatly benefited from the wisdom and experience that he has graciously shared. My association with Madame Zheng Shuling is now a decade in length, and I thank her for her trust and candor during many years of tough (and seemingly endless) negotiations in China. Our friendship is strong, based on mutual respect and a shared commitment to save the giant panda. Many other Chinese officials of the Ministry of Construction contributed to my understanding of panda conservation and management, and I thank them all. Among my other Chengdu colleagues I am grateful to Dr. He Guangxin for additional mentoring and joyful camaraderie. I also acknowledge the dedicated assistance of Xiong Wei who has helped me in so many ways in Chengdu and Atlanta as interpreter, advisor, and friend. For medical and nutritional advice I thank Yang Zhi and Zhong Shunlong.

On the domestic side, I thank my colleague and friend, Professor Donald Lindburg, coordinator of San Diego's Giant Panda Conservation Program. Dr. Lindburg sponsored our initial research in Chengdu, helping us to locate a niche in the panda research network. Needless to say, I have great admiration for his benchmark work on giant panda biology and behavior. The San Diego Zoo itself has been a lifelong source of inspiration to me. During my childhood I visited the zoo often with my family, and it never ceased to amaze and enlighten. As a native San Diegan, I take great pride in the zoo's many contributions to panda biology and conservation. Strangely, when the pandas finally arrived in San Diego, it happened on my fiftieth birthday, September 10, 1996. To compound the coincidence, twenty-one years earlier (September 10, 1975) on my twenty-ninth birthday, the first giant pandas arrived in Mexico City. Am I somehow cosmically connected to giant pandas?

I take great pleasure in reflecting on the contributions of Mr. David Towne, chairman of the Giant Panda Foundation, former AZA president, long-serving director of the Woodland Park Zoo, and now president of the Woodland Park Zoological Society. Towne's political and interpersonal skills are legendary, and his credibility in China immeasurably facilitated AZA's strategic plan. As Zoo Atlanta sought approval from Chinese and American authorities, Mr. Towne was an unwavering advocate for our common cause. AZA staff played the key roles in crafting the program of long-term panda loans. I thank Syd Butler, Kris Vehrs, and Mike Hutchins for sage advice and counsel along the way. I acknowledge with respect and gratitude a decade of advice and constructive criticism provided thoughtfully by my friend Marshall Jones.

Locally, I thank Gail Eaton who helped to plan and edit this book. She also carefully selected the superb collection of photographs, many of which were taken by Zoo Atlanta photographer Joe Sebo. For their help in obtaining additional photographs I thank Dr. Ben Beck, Dr. Donald G. Lindburg, and Dr. Juan Garza. To my friends at Longstreet, especially Tysie Whitman, thanks for your patience and your guidance as we shaped the manuscript into its final form.

I am deeply indebted to my collaborators in Atlanta. Someone had to believe in the panda project from day one and make it work on the ground in China. Panda Project Coordinator Rebecca Snyder took the risks, exercised leadership, and built the bridges that made our project viable. I am grateful also to Dr. Rita McManamon who developed a strong medical and nutritional paradigm and made strong friendships among the medical community in Chengdu and Beijing. Megan Reinertsen, Sarah Bexell, Megan Wilson, Lori Tarou, Gloria Hamor, Dr. Mollie Bloomsmith, Dr. Debra Forthman, and Dr. Yu Jinping contributed many original ideas and thousands of hours to this project. Senior zoo managers Cary Burgess, Lynn Flanders, Greg Harris, Tom LaRock, Dr. Dietrich Schaaf, and Margery Waterman provided valuable planning and operational expertise. Chief Operating Officer Steve Marshall skillfully managed the design and development of the panda exhibit from start to finish. He succeeded admirably, for it is surely the best exhibit of its kind. Our outstanding panda keeper team is led by

Assistant Curator Rich Sartor who along with Wendy Gardner, Sprina Liu, and Rebecca Singer attend to every need of our precious pandas. For editorial and scheduling assistance in writing this book, I thank Gigi Kirn. And to my lovely wife Addie and my children Molly, Emily, and Sally, thank you all for tolerating me during this ordeal, and for your kind encouragement when the words wouldn't flow. I am equally grateful to my brothers Brian and Max Maple, and my parents Merrill and Evelyn Maple, who have provided a lifetime of unconditional love and support.

The Zoo Atlanta Board of Directors encouraged me to undertake this panda pilgrimage fifteen years ago, and its support has never waned. I am especially indebted to Robert Holder Jr., Llewellen P. Haden, Robert C. Petty, Jerome Russell, and Gary Thompson for their leadership of the Zoo Atlanta board during this period. Much of the detailed preparation for the panda project was executed by an *ad hoc* task force chaired by Mr. Petty and Mr. Terry Gordon. Their personal diligence has ensured that our panda program would succeed. Several of our board committees labored long and hard to prepare the zoo for pandas. David Yu, chairman of the property committee; Bill Deyo, chairman of the development committee; Harry Saunders and Terry

Harps respectively, chairmen of the Operations Committee; and John Mellott, chairman of the marketing committee, deserve recognition. To the entire Zoo Atlanta team, and a multitude of corporate, foundation, and community friends, I appreciate your commitment to the Zoo Atlanta vision. The Chinese community in Atlanta has been a special source of friendship and pride, strengthening our resolve to develop an enduring panda conservation program. I am grateful for their continuing support.

Standards have played an important role in the shaping of our panda program, and I appreciate the efforts of personnel in the U.S. Fish & Wildlife Service, especially Kenneth Stansell and Teiko Saito in the Office of Management Authority. They provided the leadership to produce challenging regulations for the importation of giant pandas. These new regulations required higher standards of operating excellence and a rigorous program of science and conservation. Thus, the bar has been raised for those institutions seeking to exhibit and study giant pandas. This trend is consistent with recent policies of the American Zoo and Aquarium Association, whose standards for affiliation and accreditation continue to advance.

It is important for the reader to understand that the small handful of zoological parks that are home to giant pandas share a common vision. That vision requires that we learn as much as we can to advance the well being and the very survival of this highly endangered mammal. We must also work together to share our findings, and generate management protocols that will unleash the full reproductive potential of this rare creature.

Giant pandas are loved, but they must also be understood. Our growing knowledge must be applied in China; it is there, in full partnership with our Chinese colleagues, that we must make our stand in support of pandakind. There is not much time to ensure that the world will be a safe place for giant pandas and the other taxa that share their fragile habitat.

As the very symbol of conservation, the giant panda is owed our best efforts and our steadfast commitment. Saving wildlife is a marathon, not a sprint. To emerge victorious, we must be resourceful, tenacious, and wise. With your support, dear readers, Zoo Atlanta will be engaged as long as it takes.

Terry L. Maple, Ph.D.
Atlanta, Georgia
July 15, 2000

# I.
# WHO ARE THESE PANDAS, ANYWAY?

Giant pandas have long been regarded as mysterious but loveable creatures. Until 1972 when Ling Ling and Hsing Hsing arrived in our nation's capital, most Americans had never seen a giant panda. I grew up in San Diego, but I never saw a giant panda among the huge population of exotic fauna at the San Diego Zoo, touted as the largest collection of wild animals in the world. Now, at the dawn of a new century, you can see giant pandas in San Diego. You can also see them in Atlanta, and soon you may see them once again at the National Zoo in Washington, D.C. Outside China, however, giant pandas are still hard to find.

The Mandarin name for giant panda is *"da xiong mao"* which means "large bear cat." The scientific name for giant pandas is *Ailuropoda melanoleuca* meaning a "cat-footed, black and white creature." The word "panda" itself is a French distortion of a Tibetan term meaning "bamboo eater." Clearly, from its earliest origins, giant pandas were shrouded in ambiguity. I've often wondered why giant pandas were not among the animals featured in the Chinese New Year cycle of rat, bull, tiger, rabbit, dragon, snake, horse, ram, chicken, monkey, dog, pig. Given its prior range throughout much of China's territory, surely the ancient Chinese knew about the panda, and yet it does not appear as a subject in ancient Chinese sculpture or art. According to Jake Page (1984), the Chinese never "mythologized" the panda, but they also didn't utilize its body parts in traditional pharmacology as they did with so many different animals, including bears. The panda's remote home at the edge of the Himalayan Mountains presumably protected the obscure creatures from discovery

# FAMILY TREE OF PANDAS, BEARS AND OTHER CARNIVORES

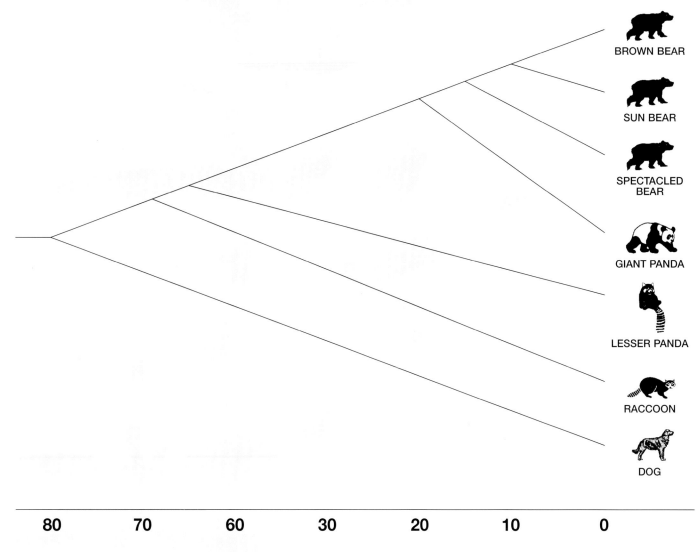

BROWN BEAR

SUN BEAR

SPECTACLED BEAR

GIANT PANDA

LESSER PANDA

RACCOON

DOG

| 80 | 70 | 60 | 30 | 20 | 10 | 0 |

## MILLIONS OF YEARS AGO

*Phylogeny of bears, giant panda, lesser panda, and raccoon from DNA hybridization data, based on the research of Dr. Oliver Ryder at San Diego's Center for Research on Endangered Species.*

HSING HSING AND LING LING, THE NATIONAL ZOO'S BELOVED GIANT PANDAS, IN THEIR OUTDOOR HABITAT.

and exploitation. We do know that giant panda pelts were received by the Emperor of China some 4,000 years ago (Page, 1984). The absence of such a charismatic creature in local legend or art is inexplicable. While there may be no official "Year of the Panda," the past 100 years is surely the "Panda's Century."

Taxonomists, the scientists who classify organisms in established categories, have argued for decades about whether the giant panda belonged in the bear or raccoon family, but recent DNA studies, including those by San Diego Zoo geneticist Oliver Ryder, suggest that they are more like bears than raccoons.

The shape of giant pandas is certainly akin to bears. They are about the same size as the American black bear (*Ursus americanus*), from 48 to 60 inches in length and up to 350 pounds (although a panda this big would surely be obese). Males are 10–20 percent larger than females. As wild giant pandas live at high elevations in the mountains of China, they are well insulated with thick coats of black and white fur. The ears, eye patches, legs and shoulders are black, while the rest of their body is white. The giant panda's black and white pattern is actually cryptic in nature, providing camouflage that makes them hard to detect. Up a tree, where they frequently go if threatened, they

Brook R. Edwards

A RARE SIGHTING OF A GIANT PANDA IN THE WILD IN CHINA, SLEEPING IN A TREE.

are practically invisible. Sitting still at a distance in a forest setting, the panda blends in with its leafy surroundings. Once revealed, its striking pelage or coat surely contributes to its charm.

A unique adaptation of the giant panda is the elongated bone (the radial sesamoid) in its wrist that protrudes from its paw like an opposable thumb. In pandas this "thumb" (labeled by some observers as a pseudothumb) is a sixth, much smaller digit. This feature enables the animals to grasp objects much like people do. They use their dexterous paws to manipulate

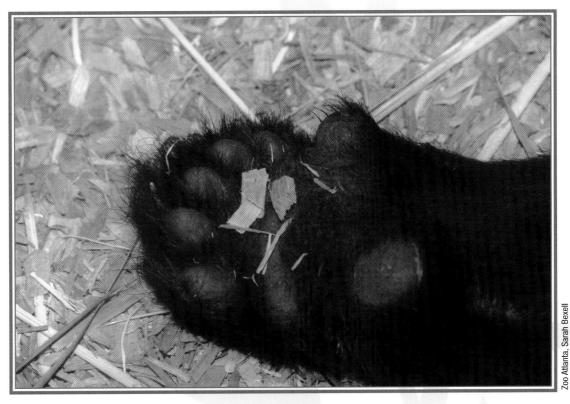

Zoo Atlanta, Sarah Bexell

THE GIANT PANDA'S PAW.

and strip bamboo, their preferred food.

Giant pandas have also been known to eat other vegetation such as gentians, irises, and crocuses, and even animal matter including fish and small rodents. It is estimated that bamboo makes up 99 percent of its diet in the wild. Bamboo is not a nutritious food, mostly comprised of fiber and cellulose. Pandas cannot digest cellulose, so they must eat twenty to forty pounds a day and forage from ten to sixteen hours a day to obtain sufficient nutrients. At best, a panda assimilates only 17 percent of the bamboo that it eats.

It is interesting to note that in times of bamboo depletion (an apparently natural phenomenon due to the bamboo flowering cycle), Chinese field workers have successfully provisioned them with morsels of meat. In captivity they have also been known to eat meat with enthusiasm. The panda seems to have acquired a herbivorous lifestyle while it has retained a basically omnivorous anatomy and physiology. More research is needed to identify subtle yet significant adaptations that have made this possible.

The longevity of giant pandas is not completely

documented. Just a few years ago, we believed that they lived into their late teens and early twenties. However, recent experience indicates that they can live much longer lives if they are cared for properly. The male giant panda Hsing Hsing at the National Zoo lived to be twenty-eight years of age. A female in China (Du Du) died on July 22, 1999, at the age of 37, a record for the species. Two other giant pandas have lived into their thirties. Qiang Qiang resided in the Shenyang Zoo until her death in 1998 at the age of 30, while Sha Sha died at 32 in the Taiyan Zoo, also in 1998. These advances in lifespan make sense if giant pandas are in fact bears, as there are many documented cases of ursids living into their forties.

The giant panda has a smaller cousin known as the lesser or red panda (*Ailurus fulgens*). Weighing 10 to 15 pounds and measuring about three feet in length, this animal is much smaller than the giant panda, resembling the North American raccoon in size and appearance. Black legs and underside, and a long, ringed tail highlight the red panda's orange-to-red woolly coat. Its face is white with orange-to-red eye patches. The red panda also lives in bamboo forests that are 3,000–12,000 feet in elevation. They are primarily arboreal and appear to be nocturnal.

They too feed almost exclusively on bamboo. One subspecies is found in the Himalayas, while the other is found in southwestern China (Sichuan and Yunnan provinces) and northern Myanmar, formerly known as Burma. Like its giant cousin, the red panda is much appreciated by zoo visitors who universally swoon at its cute and cuddly features.

All pandas have sharp teeth and powerful jaws in order to crush and masticate tough, pithy bamboo. During his service as Curator of Mammals at the London Zoo, Dr. Desmond Morris (1966) concluded that the giant panda's jaws have evolved to become a kind of "crushing machine." Animal keepers who have worked with pandas have learned to respect their power and strength. Like other bears, giant pandas can be dangerous, and they are capable of inflicting life-threatening injuries on the people who work with them. Pandas have seriously mauled some keepers, usually when the pandas have been surprised by intrusions into their enclosure. In American zoos, such as Zoo Atlanta and the San Diego Zoo, keepers are prohibited from unprotected contact with giant pandas. As with all dangerous zoo animals, giant pandas should be managed from a careful distance, through operant conditioning training methods.

Zoo Atlanta, SEBO

THE GIANT PANDA'S SMALLER COUSIN, THE RED PANDA.

By contrast, pairs or groups of keepers in China routinely enter the cages of females with offspring. Apparently, if pandas are raised in contact with human caretakers, they can be quite docile, and some giant pandas in China have been trained to perform in circus acts. Throughout China, and in some zoos, mature giant pandas have been photographed in close contact with zoo visitors. Experienced zoo curators are aware that bears have literally ripped the limbs from people who ignorantly reached through cage bars to pet them. In view of the documented danger, close contact in these ways cannot be condoned. You have to wonder how an animal so cute and compelling could arrive on earth so well equipped with lethal weaponry. The panda is, indeed, a paradox of personality and power.

What is it about pandas that renders them so cute? Why do human beings so predictably "ooh" and "aah" when they encounter them? What characteristics account for their innate charisma? These are not easy questions even for a comparative psychologist to answer, but I will try to put them into a context that makes sense to me. Part of the answer is behavioral, as pandas are playful creatures into adulthood. In addition, their locomotion is comical at times, and they often fall out of trees and climbing structures into an amusing heap (imagine Charlie Chaplin in a panda suit!). Indeed their entire repertoire of locomotor behavior may contribute to their lovable appearance. Some writers have suggested that pandas are awkward compared to other bears, but I know of no objective studies comparing them in this way. It is possible that their unique combination of cherubic attributes lead human observers to laugh at their frequent pratfalls.

In every instance when Western zoos have acquired young pandas, published accounts of their behavior reveal their propensity to play. Social play is prominent in their behavioral repertoire, but they also engage in vigorous object play with food bowls, towels, and designated play objects of any kind. One zoo provided beer kegs from a local tavern that were pushed around by the pandas, a forerunner to today's "Boomer Ball." The psychologist Harry F. Harlow used the term "peregration" to identify self-motion play in primates (Harlow & Mears, 1979). Giant pandas are also predisposed to peregration, and it is a wonderful thing to behold. True to our primate origins, human beings play throughout life. Without question, we are the most playful organism on earth. Based on what we have seen in Atlanta and Chengdu, giant pandas rank

Zoo Atlanta, SEBO

LUN LUN, THE FEMALE GIANT PANDA AT ZOO ATLANTA, RELAXES IN A HAMMOCK IN A DAYROOM.

high among the earth's most playful mammals.

The great Austrian ethologist Konrad Lorenz (1966) used the term "neoteny" to describe the infantile features of some animals and adult people. Neoteny also encompasses behavior, as prolonged playfulness is a characteristic of neoteny. Neotenous creatures and folk tend to have large heads in relation to their body size, chubby facial features, and relatively large eyes. All pandas, but especially giant pandas, fit this description.

They have chubby bodies and huge heads. Their eyes look much bigger because of the dark hairs that surround the eye, forming a kind of eye-ring or patch within the pattern of a completely white face. We have all known people whose youthful features rendered them forever cute. Because they are intrinsically childlike, we want to nurture neotenous creatures. Adult pandas look like overgrown babies to the human observer, and this phenomenon activates parental affection in people.

ZOO ATLANTA'S PANDAS YANG YANG AND LUN LUN ARE ENTHUSIASTIC PLAYMATES, RAISING RESEARCHERS' HOPES
FOR SUCCESSFUL BREEDING WHEN THEY REACH MATURITY.

Zoo Atlanta, SEBO

Cuteness is the panda's most salient characteristic. Within the panda realm are there variations in cuteness? No one really knows.

In the past, students of panda behavior have been able to observe just a few subjects, since pandas have not been available in sufficient number for serious and lengthy study. Only in China can you gather enough subjects to thoroughly investigate psychological constructs such as personality, sociality and individual differences in aggressiveness, playfulness, intelligence, etc. Fortunately, our research group has had an unusual opportunity to take a good look at a large number of giant pandas. There are a total of 24 animals in the combined collection of the Chengdu Zoo and the Chengdu Research Base of Giant Panda Breeding. Preliminary observations indicate that giant pandas, like many mammals, project distinct and measurable personalities; some are very exuberant and aggressive, whereas others are more withdrawn or stoic. However, there are many dimensions to personality that we have not yet examined in pandas.

Only formal studies, such as those other behaviorists have completed on lowland gorillas, will answer the question of how one panda personality differs from another (Gold and Maple, 1994). Information about personality may help to guide matchmaking so that compatible pandas can be successfully paired during the brief window of a mating season. In Chinese zoos and breeding centers, many pandas have proved to be incompatible, and males have often been judged "hyper-aggressive" in social situations. Many males have failed to exhibit any interest in females. There may also be common attributes of the panda that help to explain the role of personality in the expression of its unique and presumably species-typical charisma. It will also be interesting to discover how personalities endure or change in a panda's lifetime, and how males differ from females.

Although the fields of comparative psychology and ethology (defined collectively as the science of animal behavior) are not well developed in China, they will be useful disciplines when applied within Chinese zoos and breeding centers. Animal behaviorists working in China may study how certain adaptations such as a solitary lifestyle and specialized food preferences have evolved in the giant panda. It is a particularly good subject for study because the giant panda can be easily compared to other living bears and its close relative, the red panda. By training Chinese animal behaviorists, we are preparing another cadre of scientists who serve the cause of conservation. Zoo Atlanta's exchange program sends American graduate students to China and brings Chinese students to study at the Georgia Institute of Technology and Georgia State University. The students we train today will help to determine the ultimate fate of giant pandas in China. For this reason, our training programs must be designed to inform and inspire.

Fortunately, the charismatic giant panda is an attractive and highly motivating icon. I am certain that the compelling nature of the giant panda makes it easier to teach, and to influence conservation attitudes and behavior. This is why we call pandas (and some other notable creatures) "keystone" or "flagship" species. Whales are flagship species, and so are gorillas, tigers, elephants, and bald eagles. Because people are already drawn to flagship creatures, saving charismatic pandas may be a bridge to saving the whole habitat and

Zoo Atlanta, SEBO

RONG HOU, ONE OF THE CHINESE EXCHANGE RESEARCHERS, VIEWS THE PANDAS FROM THE PANDA CONTROL ROOM AT ZOO ATLANTA.

the other fauna living within it. Some flagship species are beautiful, highly intelligent, or just "living large." A flagship species isn't more important than other forms of wildlife, but it helps to motivate and activate us on behalf of all wildlife. We pay particular attention to such creatures, especially those that resemble humankind in some specific way, such as the presumed intelligence of whales or the familiar facial expressions of monkeys and apes. If charismatic megafauna didn't exist, for the sake of conservation, we would need to invent them.

Zoo Atlanta, SEBO

YANG YANG, THE MALE GIANT PANDA AT ZOO ATLANTA, RESTS COMFORTABLY ATOP THE CLIMBING STRUCTURE IN THE OUTDOOR HABITAT.

# II.
# PANDAS AND PEOPLE

Giant pandas were discovered by the Western world when Père (Father) Armand David, a French missionary, naturalist, and explorer, returned to Europe with physical evidence collected by a Chinese hunting party in 1869. David classified the animal as a member of Ursus, the bear family. Just one year later, Alphonse Milne-Edwards, a French biologist, examined the same specimen and concluded that it belonged in Procyonidae, the raccoon taxon.

In the years following its discovery, big-game hunters from the West rushed to China in hopes of being the first white man to shoot a giant panda. The elusiveness of the panda only fueled the passion of these intrepid hunters. It was the sons of Teddy Roosevelt (Theodore Jr. and Kermit) who finally brought down a giant panda in China. They shot the animal on April 13, 1929, and its remains were subsequently preserved as taxidermy in Chicago's Field Museum. These mounted specimens are still on view in the Hall of Asian Mammals, but they can never capture the grandeur of the living, breathing panda. Although other hunters sought panda material for museums, the panda's demeanor helped to turn public opinion against hunting and inspired a movement to capture pandas alive.

After 1937, with the arrival of the famed Su Lin at Brookfield Zoo in Chicago, the era of zoo pandas had arrived. In 1939, on the first Sunday of the giant panda Happy's exhibition at the St. Louis Zoo, 40,000 people came to visit him. From 1977 until 1983, thirty-six pandas were exhibited in world zoos outside China. The public response to pandas has always been remarkable.

Jessie Cohen, National Zoological Park, Smithsonian Institution

HSING HSING STRIKING AN ADORABLE POSE AT THE NATIONAL ZOO.

I first considered the prospect of seeking giant pandas for Zoo Atlanta shortly after I became zoo director in 1984. The Olympic Games were just beginning in Los Angeles. The Chinese government had agreed to send a pair of pandas to the Los Angeles Zoo during the Olympic window. This was the heyday of "rent-a-panda," when North American zoos competed to bring pandas in for short three- to six- month loans. At first there were just a few big zoos expressing interest, but in a short time the field became crowded with far too many zoos competing for a scarcity of pandas. The early panda exhibits in Los Angeles, San Francisco, Tampa, and New York were very successful. Done right, short-term panda loans seemed to work. Certainly the public enjoyed them, visiting in record numbers wherever pandas appeared.

Even though our zoo was itself just a few years removed from controversy, I began to seriously examine our prospects after our successful accreditation by the American Zoo and Aquarium Association in the spring of 1987. China had a presence in Atlanta through "ChinaTech," a program of exchange and mutual assistance operated through the Georgia Institute of Technology. Since I was a professor of psychology at Georgia Tech (on loan to the zoo), I was privy to inside information, and many of my Tech friends encouraged me to make contacts among the Chinese officials who were visiting Atlanta on a regular basis. Soon enough I was dining in Atlanta's most authentic Chinese restaurants, and every Chinese

A CHILD HOLDING A STUFFED GIANT PANDA DURING THE OPENING CEREMONIES OF THE GIANT PANDA EXHIBIT IN ATLANTA.

official who met me seemed to have the key to the giant panda vault. Throughout this phase of my education on pandas, one person kept me on point. She was Hong Kong–born Rosalind Ho, the wife of Georgia Tech mathematician Dar-Veig (David) Ho, who took me under her wing and advised me during a very sensitive period in my career. She, too, had high-level contacts in China, but she understood that a giant panda loan was a deal that only I could make. I had discovered that zoos working too closely with wealthy benefactors or ambitious local governments were getting into trouble in negotiating for pandas. Critics were getting bolder and louder as panda loans looked more and more like "cash cows" rather than conservation programs. Just three years removed from our own public crisis at Zoo Atlanta, I needed to craft an agreement on pandas that was absolutely beyond reproach. Because the giant panda was an endangered species protected by an international treaty, I knew that borrowing pandas was getting riskier with each passing transaction. When Chinese officials arrived in New York to open the Bronx Zoo's panda exhibit, I received an invitation to meet with leaders of CAZG, the Chinese Association of Zoological Gardens. My opportunity to negotiate had arrived.

I flew to New York and met them at the venerable Waldorf-Astoria Hotel. I arranged for tea and cookies for a group of eight. The bill for this modest fare was disturbing. It was my first wake-up call on the escalating cost of giant pandas. Still, the meeting was cordial and encouraging. CAZG invited me to visit Beijing as soon as possible to sign a binding agreement. Now I would have to start doing my homework on panda loans. The going fee, then as now, was $50,000 per month per panda, but there were additional costs. Chinese personnel had to accompany the animals. Their pay and their living expenses had to be paid by the host institution. Other Chinese officials would be attending the Grand Opening at our expense, and we would have to pay for insurance and for the cost of panda souvenirs made in China for sale in America. When I heard that, I took my first strong stand on the issue of trinkets: I refused them. I also argued successfully for using an American insurance firm. This also saved us a lot of money. The only thing that seemed to be nonnegotiable was the cost of pandas.

I left China in September 1987 with a short-term loan agreement. It was big news in Atlanta. The animals were scheduled to arrive in October 1988. Our

RICH SARTOR, SPRINA LIU, AND THE REST OF ZOO ATLANTA'S GIANT PANDA KEEPER STAFF CONTINUOUSLY SUPPLY FRESH BAMBOO TO YANG YANG AND LUN LUN.

exhibition would follow Toledo's, so we began to cooperate with them. I attended their splendid Grand Opening. Toledo Zoo Director Bill Dennler became a gracious mentor and friend. But sadly, Toledo became known as the city where short-term panda loans unraveled. Ironically, one of my former Zoo Atlanta colleagues, Richard Block, became a key player in the debate. Block left Zoo Atlanta to accept a position as education officer at the World Wildlife Fund in Washington, D.C. And it was WWF that first blew the whistle on "rent-a-panda." In examining the Toledo loan, WWF claimed that revenues earned from the exhibition of pandas should be used exclusively for field conservation. Block and his colleagues were tenacious. They based their argument on CITES, the Convention on International Trade of Endangered Species. The essence of the CITES treaty is that giant pandas cannot be imported from China for "primarily commercial purposes." This problem was exacerbated in the late '80s by the alarmingly large number of institutions (one of which was a commercial mall!) that were actively negotiating to exhibit giant pandas. Nobody in the zoo world believed that malls were qualified to exhibit and manage an endangered mammal such as the giant

YANG YANG AND LUN LUN SEEMED COMFORTABLE IN THEIR NEW HABITAT FROM THEIR FIRST DAY OUT.

Zoo Atlanta, SEBO

panda. Our critics began to suggest that the giant panda was in the process of being "loved to extinction." In his insightful book *The Last Panda*, George Schaller (1993) discussed why he could no longer support panda loans:

"Initially, I favored strictly regulated loans. . . . But I changed my mind after observing the greed, politics, lack of cooperation, and undisciplined scramble for pandas that characterized the whole loan program."

Eventually, the World Wildlife Fund filed suit against the U.S. Fish & Wildlife Service for failing to enforce CITES. The American Association of Zoos and Aquariums (AZA) joined the suit against the service, weighing in against one of its own members, the Toledo Zoo. It never should have come to this. Soon AZA issued a moratorium to halt short-term panda loans to AZA members until the big-picture issues could be resolved legally. In the midst of all this came the incident at Tiananmen Square in 1989. China pulled back from America. Zoo Atlanta would have to wait for its pandas, and it proved to be a long wait.

Columbus Zoo received a permit to exhibit pandas in 1992, having been grandfathered in despite the moratorium due to the timing of their 1987 agreement. But there were problems with the implementation of this loan as well, since one of the pandas had been captured in the wild. This violated the spirit, if not the principles, of CITES. I knew that Zoo Atlanta could have been grandfathered in due to the priority of our agreement, but I elected to pass, reasoning that our hard-fought battle for credibility was too important to risk, given the negative climate surrounding short-term exhibitions. In the early '90s, we began to draft a new strategy for exhibiting giant pandas: the long-term scientific loan. The San Diego Zoo was responsible for creating the new strategy, and the key contributor was Dr. Donald G. Lindburg, a highly regarded anthropologist and zoo biologist working at the San Diego Zoological Society's Center for Research on Endangered Species (CRES). In collaboration with San Diego's expert team of reproductive biologists, curators, and veterinarians, Lindburg developed a scientific program to evaluate olfaction, communication, and reproductive behavior using highly advanced scientific technology. After prolonged deliberations, the U.S. Fish & Wildlife Service accepted San Diego's proposal.

A door had been opened to acquire pandas for advanced studies of their biology and behavior, but zoos had to be invested in science to qualify, and they would have to demonstrate that the research

DR. DON LINDBURG, A BEHAVIORIST FOR THE ZOOLOGICAL SOCIETY OF SAN DIEGO, DOCUMENTS PANDA BEHAVIOR.

contributed to the survival of pandas in nature. San Diego's approach has been to intensively study the two San Diego pandas as subjects in a larger population of pandas at the Wolong Breeding Center in China. The key to this research is the coordination of studies in China and San Diego, and the compilation of pooled data. So far, it has proved to be an excellent partnership. An examination of San Diego's research priorities reveals successful collaborations in genetics, reproductive physiology, nutrition, and behavior resulting in a number of important publications jointly authored by Chinese and American scientists. At the present time, Lindburg's team is the world's most successful group of scientists at work on panda biology and conservation. They are successful in part because they are well grounded in China, with strong ties to China-based scientists, laboratories, and universities.

As this book is written, the National Zoo is poised to once again become panda exhibitors. Their twenty-seven year history of research on giant pandas may soon resume. However, panda research in this country is changed forever. There are currently three AZA institutions (Atlanta, Columbus, San Diego) working together in China to save pandas. Although Columbus doesn't currently exhibit pandas, the U.S. government regulates their remaining funding in China. This close cooperation and collaboration is a requirement of the new permit process, and it is a welcome advance. Of course, some degree of competition in research can be a good thing, for it often drives the discovery process. For that reason, the cooperating institutions have developed their own unique set of specialties, a kind of research niche. Zoo Atlanta's special research focus is socialization, the developmental process whereby pandas pass through puberty into adulthood. We are particularly interested in those variables that lead to successful socialization, reproduction, and parenting. Naturally, we must also discover why some pandas never breed. However, any developmental phenomenon must be framed in a larger biological context. For this reason we have examined reproduction in light of other scientific disciplines such as anatomy, physiology, nutrition, and medicine.

Zoo Atlanta has a history of solving mammalian breeding problems (gorillas, drill baboons, polar bears, black rhinos, Sumatran tigers, etc.) through multidisciplinary teamwork. For any species, it is highly likely that failure to breed is a function of

YANG YANG AND LUN LUN ARE CLOSE COMPANIONS WHO SPEND MUCH OF THEIR TIME TOGETHER.

many internal and external factors working together. Our commitment to a multidisciplinary study of social development should yield reliable, useful findings. In this way we hope to contribute to saving the giant panda. AZA zoos share a common commitment to conservation, education, and science. In time there will be other zoos exhibiting and researching pandas. With resources, talent, and vision, the AZA giant panda program is now fully engaged in a partnership with China.

# III.
# PANDIPLOMACY

Pandas are not delicate animals, but we have a history of treating them as if they were very delicate indeed. Certainly their rarity has contributed to this trend. In 1966 when Desmond and Ramona Morris published their famous book on pandas, only fifteen living pandas had been displayed in Western zoos, and none of these animals lived long. And yet these pandas made an impression on the public. On behalf of the Chinese Nationalist government, Madame Chiang Kai Shek made what is believed to be the first political panda gift in modern times when she sent two giant pandas to New York in 1941. (This followed by 1,315 years the very first panda gift to the Emperor of Japan.) Surely there would have been additional gifts, but the war years intervened and by 1949 the Chinese government had embraced socialism. Not surprisingly, the next gift of pandas went to Moscow in 1955. All of these pandas were captured in the wild.

During the 1960s, the Chinese government — not yet a member of the United Nations — was beginning to discover the impact of the gift of pandas. They began to regard them as a rare cultural artifact or antiquity, a living symbol of friendship and goodwill extended to the recipient state. In the twenty years from 1965 to 1985, pandas arrived in Berlin, London, Madrid, Mexico City, and Tokyo. Case by case, the art of diplomacy gave way to the science of zoo biology. The general public embraced the animals, and the media extolled their virtues in print and by image. Throughout the world, the giant panda won over the multitudes, becoming the world's most loveable creature. Pandas never fail to generate emotion in the

*continued on page 30*

# – GIANT PANDA MILESTONES –

**685**    Chinese Emperor Wu Zetian gives pandas to the Emperor of Japan.

**1869**    Père Armand David describes the giant panda from skins and bones, revealing its existence to the West.

**1929**    Roosevelt brothers kill two giant pandas for exhibition at the Field Museum of Natural History in Chicago, turning public opinion against shooting and in favor of capturing pandas.

**1937**    Captured in the wild, first giant panda is exhibited in the U.S. at Brookfield Zoo in Chicago.

**1938**    Also captured in the wild, the first giant pandas arrive at New York's Bronx Zoo.

**1941**    Nationalist China government sends two giant pandas to Bronx Zoo as gifts to the American people.

**1955**    People's Republic of China sends giant panda to Moscow.

**1957**    A second panda is sent to Moscow Zoo.

**1958**    London Zoo acquires giant panda from Austrian intermediary.

**1964**    First giant panda born in captivity at Beijing Zoo.

**1972**    Pandas arrive at the U.S. National Zoo as state gift.

**1973**    Giant pandas arrive in Japan.

Two giant pandas are given to Paris Zoo.

Two giant pandas are given to London Zoo.

**1979**    First giant pandas produced by artificial insemination in China.

# ~ GIANT PANDA MILESTONES ~

**1980**    First giant panda born outside China at Mexico City Zoo.

**1981**    Giant pandas arrive in West Berlin.

**1983**    Wolong Giant Panda Conservation Center established in China (designed by WCS; funded by WWF).

**1984**    Pandas loaned to Los Angeles Zoo for short-term exhibition during the Olympic Games.

**1988**    World Wildlife Fund sues U.S. Fish & Wildlife Service over excesses of "rent-a-panda."

**1989**    AZA issues moratorium on short-term exhibition of giant pandas by AZA member zoos.

**1993**    San Diego Zoo negotiates long-term loan of giant pandas with China's Ministry of Forestry.

Formation of AZA's Giant Panda Foundation.

Publication of George Schaller's influential book *The Last Panda*.

**1996**    Two giant pandas arrive at the San Diego Zoo.

Giant panda studbook is published.

**1999**    Two giant pandas arrive at Zoo Atlanta.

Panda Hua Mei is born at San Diego Zoo by artificial insemination.

Panda Hsing Hsing dies at the National Zoo at the age of 29.

**2000**    San Diego Zoo and World Wildlife Fund host world conference on Giant Panda Conservation.

National Zoo submits application to U.S. Fish & Wildlife Service for importation of two Giant Pandas.

Chinese government and WWF begin third census of giant panda population in the wild.

human onlooker. They are unique in their ability to produce this powerful effect.

By the early 1980s, according to Schaller, 101 pandas had been delivered to zoos (most of them Chinese zoos) after their capture in the Baoxing region of China. Baoxing is very close to the major city of Chengdu, the departure point for the earlier Western collecting expeditions in the 1930s. As we enter the twenty-first century, there are 132 giant pandas in captivity, 55 males and 71 females, plus six new babies at the Wolong Breeding Center whose sex was undetermined at press time. They currently reside in 32 zoos and breeding centers. Only fifteen giant pandas live outside China at the present time.

The story of Zoo Atlanta's pandas is closely connected to President Jimmy Carter. For many years, I admired him from afar. In the late seventies, I tried to figure out a way to play softball with him, but an invitation never arrived. (President Carter had developed a reputation as a fine slow pitcher and, as a former baseball player, I wanted a chance to face him.) As it turned out, I didn't meet him until after I became Atlanta's zoo director in 1984, long after I had retired from the softball diamond. It was Carter's son Chip who first introduced us one day as Chip and his small children visited the zoo with President Carter and his wife Rosalynn. It was a great thrill to show them the rapidly changing new Atlanta zoo. On this occasion, I became aware of President Carter's passion for the natural world. He was very well informed on environmental issues, and he expressed a complete understanding of Zoo Atlanta's wildlife vision.

Once I began to seriously pursue the acquisition of giant pandas, I realized that President Carter would be the most effective advocate for our initiative. Revered in China for restoring full diplomatic relations with the Chinese government, he still had good contacts among the Chinese leadership. In my earliest conversations with him, it was clear that he also had a profound understanding of Chinese culture and character. I listened to him carefully, as I had a lot to learn about dealing with China. With President Carter's support, we would have the opportunity to go right to the top with our request. At that time, short-term panda loans were still possible, and I was certain that we had crafted a plan that would benefit panda conservation and public education. I discussed our ideas with President Carter in his office at the Carter Center, and he agreed to make a request on our behalf during his

Zoo Atlanta, Rebecca Snyder

LUN LUN, STILL A TODDLER, RESTS IN THE OUTDOOR YARD AT THE CHENGDU RESEARCH BASE FOR GIANT PANDA BREEDING.

Zoo Atlanta, SEBO

FORMER PRESIDENT JIMMY CARTER AND ROSALYNN CARTER GREET THE HONORABLE LI ZHAOXING,
AMBASSADOR OF THE PEOPLE'S REPUBLIC OF CHINA, AT THE PANDA ARRIVAL CELEBRATION AT ZOO ATLANTA.

next visit to China. In China, he confided to Chairman Deng Xiaoping that while other political leaders had received them in their home states, pandas had not been exhibited in Georgia. Carter suggested to Deng that he would "lose face" if the pandas didn't come to Atlanta. Soon thereafter I received an invitation to visit China.

After our short-term panda loan had been approved by the State Council in Beijing in 1987, we hit the brick wall of litigation. With the American Zoo and Aquarium Association supporting the World Wildlife Fund's 1988 lawsuit against the U.S. Fish & Wildlife Service, this did not seem to be a good time for Zoo Atlanta to buck the trend. We backed away from "rent-a-panda" and never looked back. When I shared my decision with President Carter at the time, he concurred. I took great comfort in this. We agreed that Zoo Atlanta's panda exhibition would have to be ethically sound.

In the midst of the controversy over "rent-a-panda," I began to think about how we fit into the new realities in China. By then, we had been sitting on our short-term loan for several years with no hope of reactivating it, certainly not during the AZA moratorium. I wondered whether short-term loans would ever again be acceptable. The long-term loan model appeared to be a better way to exhibit pandas, and it provided for more sustained conservation support in China. Given the strength of our scientific program, a long-term scientific project was an opportunity tailor-made for Zoo Atlanta. In addition, I surmised our chances might be improved by the fact that Atlanta would be hosting the Centennial Olympic Games in the summer of 1996. Surely the Chinese would recognize the Olympics as a fitting occasion for a panda arrival, and this might speed up the approval process. And so we began a lengthy negotiation with the Chinese government.

In 1993 a consortium of zoos formed to see if giant panda loans could be reinvented in an acceptable form. Busch Gardens and San Diego had pioneered the long-term loan strategy and we were all anxious to see if there was further opportunity to develop a win/win panda loan program. One of the early meetings took place at the Carter Center in Atlanta at my invitation. One of the President's trusted associates, Joe Giordano, shared the Center's experiences working in China. It was his contention that our goal to closely monitor U.S.-funded panda-conservation projects in China was entirely feasible. At this meeting, too, we learned more about the approach that San Diego was taking to gain approval with the U.S. Fish & Wildlife Service. However, in 1993 we were still awaiting new regulations for panda imports. San Diego was still trying to execute their agreement under the terms of the previous panda regulations. In addition, the AZA moratorium on short-term loans was still in effect. No one knew whether the AZA board of directors would approve any kind of panda loan.

In the midst of this tension, Dave Towne was elected to the AZA board. The following year the electorate chose me to serve on the board. For seven years, Dave and I found ourselves in the eye of a hurricane of controversy. Just one year later, I began to feel the bumps. I attempted to reestablish Zoo Atlanta's relationship to CAZG, the Chinese Association of Zoological Gardens. Chinese zoos had always reported to their country's Ministry of

Jessie Cohen, National Zoological Park, Smithsonian Institution

HSING HSING IN 1979 ENJOYING VEGETABLES AND A FOOD PAN IN THE PANDA HOUSE AT THE NATIONAL ZOO.

Construction, and this ministry had a long history of arranging panda loans for zoos outside China. Madame Zheng Shuling, a high-ranking deputy director in the Ministry of Construction, agreed to see me in Beijing during the spring of 1994. Unfortunately, this was not a great time to be in China. The very day I arrived, China began lobbing missiles in the vicinity of Taiwan. There was a distinct chill in the Beijing air. I met Madame Zheng at the cavernous Ministry of Construction (home of the Chinese Association of Zoological Gardens) accompanied by Zoo Atlanta's consulting architect, Gary Lee. Mr. Lee is a Chinese-American zoo designer with just enough Cantonese vocabulary to understand some of the Mandarin that Madame Zheng was hurling at me. He took copious notes, so I would always remember the moment. It was immediately clear that Madame Zheng was ready to rumble. I had expected to work out the details of Zoo Atlanta's panda loan, but instead I took the heat for every recent transgression by our government, from espionage to support for Taiwan, and especially our haughty attitudes about conservation. Unprepared for the tongue-lashing, I was a convenient scapegoat for the actions of the U.S. Fish & Wildlife Service just a few months prior to my visit.

Their proposed regulations had not been well received by the Ministry of Construction, and our Chinese colleagues needed to vent their emotions.

Many of my AZA colleagues agreed with the principle that panda loan funds should be prioritized so that field conservation received a significantly greater share, as much as 80 percent — as initially recommended by the U.S. Fish & Wildlife Service. This meant that the Chinese Ministry of Forestry, which manages the national parks and reserves, would receive nearly all the money. Since Forestry also loaned pandas to zoos (Forestry loaned the San Diego Zoo pandas), the developing competition between the two Ministries was not helpful. While their entrepreneurial spirit was consistent with positive economic changes in China, it also contributed to criticism that panda loans were more commerce than conservation. Understandably, Construction officials were livid about the proposed 80/20 distribution model. Given the needs, interests, and potential of China's zoological parks, I had to agree that the provisions were shortsighted and unfair to our zoo colleagues.

Madame Zheng was certain that there were only four pairs of pandas available for American zoos, and she was equally certain that under the terms of the proposed system of regulations, none of them would be going west anytime soon. She blamed our government, and she blamed AZA. And if I didn't do something about it, she was going to blame me, too. In her three days of criticism, she made one final, salient point that summarized the entire problem. It was a matter of trust, she opined: "You Americans just don't trust us." I was so demoralized by the end of the day I went back to my hotel and made plans to fly home a day early. I couldn't remember a worse day in China, exacerbated by intermediaries who were trying to deter me from my relationship to Construction. I had entered an uncomfortable quandary, and it was time to get out. I was certain that my hotel line was being tapped, and my paranoia was out of control.

During the fifteen-hour flight back to the United States, I had plenty of time to ruminate. Gary Lee and I endlessly discussed the meaning and significance of my experience. Gary was confident that something good would come of it. By the time we reached Los Angeles, I was certain that I shared Madame Zheng's conclusion that the zoos of China had been unfairly maligned, and I readied myself to deliver a strong message to my fellow zoo directors. For an entire year I worked to encourage a consensus among my col-

leagues. We needed to support our fellow zoo professionals in China, I proposed. It was clear to me that we also needed to help upgrade the management of the 100 giant pandas living in Chinese zoos and breeding centers. This population could function as leverage against extinction if the wild population crashed. In 1994, we were still debating the accuracy of the studbook, which was slow to incorporate a complete set of data from China. Nevertheless, it appeared that the Chinese zoo population was in trouble. Obviously, China's zoos needed our financial support.

The following year, I did my best to argue for balance in the proposed policies of the U.S. Fish & Wildlife Service. On behalf of the Panda Foundation and AZA, Towne and I appealed to Dr. Ulie Seal of the prestigious International Union of the Conservation of Nature (IUCN) Conservation Breeding Specialists Group (CBSG). We asked Dr. Seal to independently evaluate the panda situation and give us advice on how to structure support in China. After some initial resistance, he agreed to participate, but only if he could select "unbiased" evaluators from non-panda-seeking institutions. Except for the participation of Don Lindburg, we accepted his conditions. In his new role as Panda SSP Coordinator, Dr. Lindburg was too important to be left out of the workshop. True to his scientific credentials, Lindburg managed to participate as an objective nonpartisan, and his expertise proved invaluable.

CBSG's report, based on workshops in Chengdu and Wolong, established at last that conservation in China required both field and zoo approaches. In fact, some of the zoo-based tools and techniques would actually benefit field conservation. For example, the principles of zoo medicine would help field workers to evaluate the health of wild animals. Seal's team, led by Dr. David Wildt, contributed to the eventual refinement of Fish & Wildlife's approach to panda conservation. When the revised regulations were announced on August 26, 1998, the language was more flexible and the requirements more agreeable to our colleagues at the CAZG. We had finally arrived at a reasonable consensus on how to proceed in China. It had taken a long, long time to resolve, but the Fish & Wildlife Service had succeeded in producing a breakthrough document. This day was a genuine turning point for AZA's panda plan.

San Diego finally received their pandas in September 1996, the culmination of a mysterious power struggle within China. We offered assistance to our colleagues in San Diego, asking President Carter to intervene on their behalf. Of course, San Diego had their own powerful political support from California Senator Dianne Feinstein, whom as mayor of San Francisco established the first "sister" relationship to a Chinese city. The mayor of Shanghai at the time just happened to be Jiang Zemin, the current president of China.

The political pressure was particularly strong during an Olympic year. In fact, there was talk about the San Diego pandas passing through Atlanta for the Olympic window and then moving on to San Diego. The Chinese government actually approved the plan and then issued a press release to confirm it. This was not what San Diego and Zoo Atlanta had in mind. If the Olympics could bring the pandas to San Diego we were eager to try, but the Olympic window would have resulted in a short-term exhibition, and we couldn't agree to that. On March 30, 1996, I wrote an editorial in the *Atlanta Journal-Constitution*, which emphasized that Zoo Atlanta was interested in long-term exhibition only. Nothing came of the Olympic opportunity, but the two Ministries agreed to sign off on the San Diego loan and the pandas were on their way. September 10, 1996, was a historic day for San

Diego, and it effectively launched the AZA giant panda program.

Despite criticism that as AZA president his panda work for the Foundation was in conflict, Dave Towne managed to wear both hats in 1998. When he agreed to continue in both roles, I knew that our momentum would accelerate. We desperately needed his skillful leadership at the helm of this delicate program, and Towne's AZA presidency actually contributed to his effectiveness in China. With one pair of pandas in the country, it was time to test the new importation process. Somehow, someway, Zoo Atlanta had moved to the front of the line. We had a contract, and we had developed an exemplary research plan. With one year of work in China accomplished, we were ready to submit our credentials to the feds. I was confident that we would qualify for an import permit, but there were some worrisome details to overcome. Under the new policies, a greater percentage of the money returned to China had to be earmarked for priority field conservation. The Ministry of Construction was agreeable to this new ratio. But Zoo Atlanta had no working relationship with the Ministry of Forestry, who would be overseeing the field conservation work, and there-

fore no plan for the use of our money. As a result, we had to find a suitable program of field conservation that could be supported by our funds. We accomplished this by hiring a Chinese citizen trained in conservation biology, Yu Jinping, who is sufficiently skilled to evaluate field programs and recommend refinements.

Our application to import two giant pandas was approved on June 15, 1999, by the U.S. Fish and Wildlife Service, coincidentally the fifteenth anniversary of my appointment as Director of Zoo Atlanta. Officials of the U.S. Fish & Wildlife Service helped us to deliver the news in a historic press conference held at the zoo. The Service wanted to make sure that the public understood the conditions of the import permit; namely, that Zoo Atlanta was obligated to seriously study these pandas, and support only meaningful conservation work in China. We were delighted when the local and national media immediately began to tell the complex conservation and science story.

After the successful press conference, we began preparations to fly the pandas to Atlanta. We committed to raising the money and building a world-class exhibit, even though some issues remained unresolved. We had confidence in our plan, and we

Zoo Atlanta, SEBO

DR. TERRY MAPLE PROUDLY DISPLAYS THE SIGNED PERMIT TO IMPORT GIANT PANDAS. KENNETH STANSELL OF THE U.S. FISH AND WILDLIFE SERVICE AND SYDNEY BUTLER, EXECUTIVE DIRECTOR OF THE AMERICAN ZOO AND AQUARIUM ASSOCIATION, PARTICIPATED IN THE SIGNING CEREMONY.

FORMER PRESIDENT JIMMY CARTER SHOWS HIS EXCITEMENT OVER THE IMPENDING ARRIVAL OF GIANT PANDAS AT ZOO ATLANTA.

remained focused on our goal. We were actually ready to receive the pandas as early as June, but the scheduled arrival kept slipping back due to paperwork problems. Final approvals were moving very slowly in China, and I had no guarantee that Forestry, the last required signature, would approve in a timely fashion. For this reason, I engaged the process from two directions. I kept working with my contacts in China at the appropriate scientific and technical levels. Simultaneously I worked the project from the top. I still feared that Ministry infighting might stall our progress.

# IV.
# PANDAMONIUM

I'm not sure that I will ever fully understand how the giant pandas were finally cleared for their flight to Atlanta. As we counted down to the final thirty days, we were fighting paperwork battles on all fronts. We needed visas for the pilots, landing rights approvals from several Chinese agencies, and the final sign-off by the Ministry of Forestry on our import permit. Every day there was a vexing new problem that we had to solve without delay. The stress was palpable around our Zoo Atlanta offices.

Two key people worked some last-minute magic for us in the final days before the flight. Chinese Ambassador to the United States Mr. Li Zhaoxing had visited the zoo during a speech-making trip to Atlanta. We arranged an early-morning breakfast for him in the panda exhibit itself. It was a spectacular presentation, and he was most impressed with the quality of our facilities. After a thorough tour of our panda night house, he agreed to help us meet our timeline. With Ambassador Li's assistance and coordination from Wu Jurong at the Houston Consulate, the paperwork finally began to move in China. We tried to make an October window, but it soon became apparent that the 50-year celebration of the People's Republic was going to preempt everything in China for a while. Our UPS partners agreed to establish one more window for the flight. I was told that we were running out of time due to the impending Christmas business schedule, which would tie up all the planes, including our beloved Panda Express. We agreed that November 5 was the last opportunity to bring the pandas to Atlanta before the millennium.

# The Atlanta Journal

*Covers Dixie Like The Dew*

TODAY'S NEWS

ONLINE @ AJC.COM — MONDAY, OCT. 25, 1999 — TO SUBSCRIBE: 404-522-4141

# Here come the pandas

## Chinese officials approve visit to Zoo Atlanta

**Playtime:** Yang Yang (left) and Lun Lun take a moment for some panda talk as they face each other on top of the panda jungle gym at the Chengdu Research Base of Giant Panda Breeding in southwest China.

By Marcia Kunstel
and Joseph Albright
STAFF CORRESPONDENTS

**Beijing** — The giant pandas Lun Lun and Yang Yang took a giant step closer to Zoo Atlanta today, when their Chinese keepers finally got high-level government approval to dispatch them halfway across the world for a 10-year stay in Atlanta.

Two officials of Zoo Atlanta were informed today of the decision while visiting the pandas' current stomping grounds, the Chengdu Research Base of Giant Panda Breeding.

"We have just had an absolutely wonderful day," said researcher Sarah Bexell.

Whether the panda pair will travel on schedule and arrive in Atlanta on Thursday, however, was less clear.

"If everything is under control, that is our schedule," said Yu

Any further delays and we would have to wait until the spring of 2000.

During this final waiting period, we once again ran into last-minute complications in the approval process. It was here that we received powerful assistance from the office of U.S. Senator Max Cleland. Senator Cleland's status with the Clinton Administration ensured that we would have access to our top Embassy personnel within China. Senator Cleland responded immediately to my call for help, and used his influence with our Embassy in Beijing to facilitate all the transactions that were necessary to fly on time. I will forever be indebted to him for his timely intervention. President Carter, Senator Cleland, Ambassador Li, Wu Jurong, and a multitude of warriors at UPS: these were some of the true heroes of our flight out of China. Of course, I would also single out my crack senior staff for praise, particularly Gail Eaton, our marketing director and Greg Harris, our development director, who mediated the sensitive negotiations between UPS managers

"FLIGHT ATTENDANTS" WHO CARED FOR THE PANDAS DURING THE LONG FLIGHT INCLUDED DR. ZHONG SHUNLONG OF THE CHENGDU ZOO, DR. RITA MCMANAMON OF ZOO ATLANTA, AND DR. YANG ZHI OF THE CHENGDU RESEARCH BASE FOR GIANT PANDA BREEDING.

# – PANDA ARRIVAL SCHEDULE –

| EVENT | CHINA TIME | ATLANTA TIME |
| --- | --- | --- |
| Pandas depart Chengdu | November 4, 2:00 A.M. | November 3, 1:00 P.M. |
| Pandas depart Beijing | November 5, 6:10 A.M. | November 4, 5:10 P.M. |
| Arrive in Anchorage for refueling | | November 5, 12:09 A.M. |
| Depart Anchorage | | November 5, 2:40 A.M. |
| Press conference set-up begins | | November 5, 3:30 A.M. |
| Media crews begin arriving at Zoo/UPS hangar | | November 5, 4:00 A.M. |
| Press conference at UPS hangar begins | | November 5, 8:30 A.M. |
| Pandas arrive in Atlanta | | **November 5, 9:30 A.M.** |
| "Pandacade" leaves UPS hangar | | November 5, 10:25 A.M. |
| "Pandacade" arrives at Zoo Atlanta/Pandas unloaded | | November 5, 10:50 A.M. |
| Zoo Atlanta giant panda footage released to the media | | November 5, 4:30 P.M. |
| Last media crew leaves Zoo Atlanta | | November 5, 8:30 P.M. |

THERE WERE TEARS OF JOY AND RELIEF AT HARTSFIELD AIRPORT WHEN THE FIRST CRATE
CONTAINING YANG YANG WAS UNLOADED FROM THE "PANDA EXPRESS."

UPS WORKERS UNLOAD THE CRATE CONTAINING LUN LUN AT HARTSFIELD INTERNATIONAL AIRPORT.
IF YOU LOOK CLOSELY, YOU CAN SEE LUN LUN PEERING OUT THROUGH THE TOP OF THE CRATE.

A JOYFUL FLIGHT CREW EMERGED FROM THE "PANDA EXPRESS" AFTER A 17-HOUR JOURNEY
TO A HUGE WELCOMING CROWD AT HARTSFIELD INTERNATIONAL AIRPORT.

and Chinese officials literally day and night.

Early in our negotiations with United Parcel Service, we had learned that we would have only three seats on the plane for zoo personnel. It had been easy for me to decide that this was no occasion for ceremony; I assigned the seats to our devoted Zoo veterinarian, Dr. Rita McManamon, and two veterinary colleagues from Chengdu. Rita spent several weeks in China before the

flight, working with our Chinese colleagues to reduce the stress of travel for our precious pandas. In the months prior to the pandas' departure, we also relied upon Zoo Atlanta conservation educator Sarah Bexell to help generate the panda logistics. With Rita and Sarah in China, I was certain that we would meet our timeline.

Our friends at UPS had labored long and hard on a detailed logistical plan that required the utmost

POLICE ESCORT THE "PANDACADE" FROM HARTSFIELD AIRPORT TO ZOO ATLANTA ON NOVEMBER 5, 1999.

precision. This was hard to do, since they would be flying into and out of Beijing for the first time. UPS decided to route the flight though Anchorage, Alaska, which required special permission to fly in Russian air space. The company prepared two special 767 cargo jets painted with pandas that were christened the "Panda Express." UPS planners left no stone unturned, as one of the planes was a backup for the other. They were the most magnificent airplanes I have ever seen.

The long flight from Beijing to Atlanta would become one of the true highlights of Dr. McManamon's distinguished career. It was indeed a medical flight, but there was no avoiding the ceremony that erupted wherever the spectacular "Panda Express" appeared. In Beijing, Rita and her medical colleagues struggled to deter a virtual

SPECIALLY MARKED UPS "PANDA EXPRESS" PACKAGE CARS DELIVERED THE PANDAS TO ZOO ATLANTA.

Zoo Atlanta, Jim Fitts

flock of photographers who wanted to get closer to the departing pandas. In Anchorage, midpoint of the flight, hundreds of onlookers greeted the plane, while our celebrated pandas made the front page of local newspapers.

Flying at 39,000 feet, Chengdu to Beijing to Anchorage to Atlanta, enduring two full days of intense movement and the tedious, between-flight, downtime, was exhausting for everyone involved. The three veterinarians shared the responsibility of catering to the pandas' every need. Like highly trained flight attendants, they fed them bamboo, checked their customized crates (designed by zoo managers, built by UPS at a cost of $7500 per crate), inspected their faces for signs of fatigue or dehydration, and generally assessed their health and well-being every fifteen to twenty minutes. They took copious notes, in Chinese and in English, to record every significant observation and event. Under these conditions, there could be no productive sleep time for our medical staff. They were focused and attentive to every detail of the protocol. According to Rita, everyone on the aircraft recognized the importance of this flight. A sense of mission, camaraderie, and teamwork prevailed. To UPS and Zoo Atlanta, these pandas were the most precious of cargo, and those who managed the details of their flight felt the pressure of the awesome responsibility. In Atlanta, we could only worry and fuss, counting down the hours as they sped toward our reunion. Any time a creature is translocated from one zoo to another, there is reason to plan and to worry. Under the best conditions, wild animals do not suffer movement gladly. One million dollars of insurance (required by the Chinese) provided no comfort. We couldn't allow ourselves to contemplate any accident or injury to our pandas. It was truly unthinkable.

On November 5 the pandas arrived in Atlanta aboard the Panda Express, none the worse for the thirty-two-hour flight from Chengdu, a distance of more than 6,000 miles. (Our veterinary friends seemed a bit tired by comparison!) As the magnificent Panda Express approached the hangar at Hartsfield International Airport, which was jammed full of well-wishers and friends, airport water cannons streamed a two-barrel salute over the bow of the incoming jet. Rita and her Chinese colleagues Yang Zhi and Zhong Shunlong beamed as they greeted the throng. Veteran UPS Flight Captain Bob Peterson told us, "It was a beautiful flight. There were no clouds the entire way." As expected, United Parcel Service managed the flawless delivery of two distinguished ambassadors for giant pandakind. This was indeed a unique day, unlike any other in the zoo's long history. Tears of joy punctuated the sense of pride. Zoo Atlanta would have its pandas after all.

In the end, it was preparation and careful planning, experience and training, patience, teamwork, and the leadership of highly qualified personnel that triumphed over every kind of logistical impediment and diversion. Our pandas Lun Lun and Yang Yang deserve some credit, too. They calmly accepted the inconveniences and demonstrated their unique durability. At long last, their mission to educate and inspire humankind was underway in Atlanta.

Zoo Atlanta, SEBO

LUN LUN AND YANG YANG EXPLORE THE CLIMBING STRUCTURE IN OUTDOOR HABITAT ONE.

# V.
# OBSERVING PANDAS

Watching pandas (one of my favorite activities) is not the same as observing pandas, although the panda observers that I know surely enjoy their work. Scientific observation requires a system and a method. Observation of this type is objective, without bias. Scientific observation seeks the truth. When "zoo-goers" watch pandas, our minds tend to wander (and wonder). That's the fun of it! In contrast, scientists observe with focus and discipline. They must gather data in a certain way, at a certain time, and they must accurately record specific, defined events or behaviors. A lot of historical information on the panda is from casual watching, and it has led to many ambiguous anecdotes. Until recently, we had little information about pandas to combat the misinformation. Today we have collected an impressive array of objective data from zoo studies, and a growing amount of field data. Gradually, an accurate picture of panda biology and behavior is emerging.

The first task of the animal behaviorist is to describe the complete behavioral repertoire of the species in question. This list of behaviors is known as an "ethogram." National Zoo scientist Dr. Devra Kleiman published the first complete ethogram for the giant panda in 1983. The Kleiman ethogram comprised some seventy behaviors, but this number has increased as a result of subsequent work by scientists at the San Diego Zoo and Zoo Atlanta. An ethogram is never truly exhaustive, nor is it the last word in defining behaviors. Replication (repeating a study by a different observer in a different setting) always leads to refinements and changes of meaning or interpretation. From a scientific point of view, the proliferation of panda research settings is likely to produce confirmation and new discovery at a much faster rate. Some pooling of behavioral data is desirable, but systematic replication should be entirely independent. For example, we cannot establish the moment that young pandas begin to exert autonomy until we have observed many panda mother-infant pairs across different settings. Since a baby panda is being observed in San Diego, it will be useful to compare that animal's development with any offspring produced in Atlanta or elsewhere.

When you investigate a new species, it is important to establish a basic pattern of activity. Some animals neatly fall into simple categories — for example, nocturnal vs. diurnal. However, giant pandas are more difficult to classify. They are active both day and night, alternating their eating and their sleeping, punctuated with play if they are housed socially. Activity also varies with age, with younger animals more active than older ones. Some studies have suggested gender differences in activity — for example, wild male pandas appear to have larger home ranges than females. Our own studies of young pandas at Chengdu and Zoo Atlanta indicate that males initiate more play and spend more time playing than do females. Kleiman in

Zoo Atlanta, SEBO

REBECCA SINGER, GIANT PANDA KEEPER, OBSERVES
ZOO ATLANTA'S PANDAS FROM ABOVE.

# -TABLE 5-1-
## DIFFERENCES BETWEEN WILD AND CAPTIVE GIANT PANDAS
(Modified with permission from Son Yanling)

| ITEMS | | WILD IN CHINA | CAPTIVE IN CHINA |
|---|---|---|---|
| Living environment | — | Natural habitat | Enclosures |
| Pressures | — | Natural selection | Artificial selection |
| Parasites | — | Common | Treatable |
| Lifestyle | — | Solitary | Single, pair, or group |
| Home range | — | mean = 5 sq. km. | Generally small |
| Migration | — | Vertical annually | Unable to migrate |
| Daily foraging | — | ten hours/day | Four hours/day |
| Food | — | Leaves, shoots & bamboo twigs | bamboo, corn bread, apple, milk, eggs |
| Activity cycle | — | Two peaks (0300–0600; 1500–1900) | Affected by time of feeding (peaks 1–2 hrs. before feeding) |
| Social structure | — | Male home range overlaps one or more females | No opportunity |
| Competition | — | Males fight to mate with females at site | Paired by caretakers |
| Mating habits | — | Normal for species | Most animals do not mate |
| Weaning | — | Natural at 8–9 mos. | Set by caretakers at 3–4 mos. |
| Leaves mother | — | 1.5–2.5 years | 3–4 months |

her 1983 study also suggested that giant pandas might be nocturnal, but in view of the small sample size, she regarded her findings as tentative at best. It may turn out that giant pandas are essentially crepuscular, meaning very active in the early morning and early evening hours, or they may be essentially "polycyclic" with regard to activity. Data from the field indicate that giant pandas are most active early in the morning and at twilight. This is an issue that needs to be settled and, given the larger number of giant pandas now available for study, it will be resolved in the near future.

We have already discussed the playful tendencies of young pandas. They engage in play with their mothers, objects, conspecific peers, and their keepers if they have the opportunity. In social play they chase each other and push each other down. The playmate is grasped and gently bitten as they roll around together on the ground or in a climbing structure. They sometimes vocalize in play, but their behavior is restrained. It is rough-and-tumble play, but no one gets hurt. If any animal gets hurt, the pair has crossed the boundary from play to aggression.

People who watch pandas love to see them play, but the animals are interesting no matter what they are doing. I have watched them in Atlanta, Los Angeles, New York, San Diego, San Francisco, Tampa, Toledo, and Washington, D.C. I have also seen pandas in Berlin, London, and in Beijing, Chengdu, and Hong Kong. In many of these locations, I arrived when they were napping. Because of their unique coloration and their roly-poly appearance, people seem to enjoy them even when they are asleep. At such times, visitors universally exclaim: "They're so cute!" A common remark on such occasions is, "Hey, he's not asleep, he's wiggling his ears!" Folks just love to look at pandas.

The giant panda is uniquely adapted to lie on its back and to use its protruding tummy as a plate. Some bear species assume this position when they are nursing their offspring. When pandas lean back and consume bamboo in this way, it is sheer cuteness. In this position, the visitor also sees their full face, glimpses their powerful teeth, gets a good look at their workable thumb, and hears the crunching of the bamboo in their awesome jaws. I particularly like to watch the giant pandas eat. Fortunately for most zoo visitors, and owing to their dependence on bamboo, they always seem to be eating.

Giant pandas are known to communicate by vocalizations and the release of strong scent marks. As classified by Devra Kleiman, their vocal repertoire

Zoo Atlanta, SEBO

THE DAYROOMS IN THE GIANT PANDA EXHIBIT AT ZOO ATLANTA ALLOW VISITORS UP-CLOSE VIEWING OF THE PANDAS THROUGH GLASS. THE CLIMATE-CONTROLLED DAYROOMS ALLOW LUN LUN AND YANG YANG TO REMAIN ON EXHIBIT DURING EXTREME HEAT AND COLD.

LUN LUN SLUMPS INTO A COMFORTABLE POSITION AND USES HER BELLY AS HER "PLATE."

consists of bleats, chirps, moans, barks, growls, roars, squeals, honks, and nonvocal jaw clapping. Bleating appears to be a short-distance contact call, which is also commonly emitted during the spring breeding season. As one might expect, it has been compared to the sound of a goat or sheep. Vocalizations of all kinds occur primarily during aggressive or reproductive interactions within the breeding season. Neonates, or newborns, make a specialized high-pitched call that brings attention from the mother.

Scent marking may be the most important mode of communication among giant pandas. They secrete a thick, sticky fluid from the anogenital glands, imparting information that is discovered by other pandas. Kleiman identified five distinct postures associated with scent marking in giant pandas. Recent work at the San Diego Zoo has confirmed the importance of scent marking in this species. The San Diego team also demonstrated that giant pandas were capable of differentiating between scent samples. There is evidence that scent marking functions to deter competing males, and to attract mates to ovulating females.

One of my students Rebecca Snyder's first work in Chengdu was designed to learn more about abnormal behavior patterns that interfere with mating in pandas. A majority of females in the Chinese zoo and breeding center populations do not exhibit a normal behavioral estrus (the period of time during which females will accept males for breeding). Her study monitored behavior and urinary hormone output during the 1997, 1998, and 1999 breeding seasons in Chengdu. Snyder's preliminary results indicate that a smaller subset of the entire list of "estrus behaviors" is sufficient to predict estrus, but estrus varies considerably among females. She also advised that young male pandas should be given contact with receptive females to encourage the development of appropriate mating behaviors. Isolation from mature partners may contribute to male indifference.

While our work on the mating habits of pandas continues, our primary focus is the socialization process. To this end, we are fundamentally interested in how pandas become fully functioning adults. The reproductive failure of many zoo pandas in China resembled the failures in many American zoos just twenty years ago. In the early eighties, the lowland gorilla was a high-profile failure in American zoos. No one really knew why gorillas weren't breeding. In our book *Gorilla Behavior* (1982), Michael Hoff and I examined the variables that affect reproduction in this taxon. It is a complicated issue but then, as now, socialization issues were paramount. Many gorillas had been taken from their mothers at an early age and raised by human caretakers. Depending on the degree of contact with humans, these animals experienced a continuum of conditions, from social deprivation to isolation. As we learned from the work of Harry F. Harlow, such conditions can lead to the development of abnormal and self-destructive behaviors: stereotyped behaviors, hyper-aggression, reduced libido, pathological fear, and abusive or neglectful parenting in those few that successfully reproduce. Harlow's pioneering research on rhesus monkeys led to other developmental studies of social mammals including great apes, big cats, wolves, and black and grizzly bears. Parenting by the mother has proved to be the key variable in the development of appropriate social behaviors for a variety of mammals.

In 1996, the behaviorists Huang, Huang, and Lindburg examined the reproductive records and developmental history of seventeen male pandas more than six years of age in Chinese zoos and breeding centers. At the time of that study, only one captive-born male had sired offspring. Furthermore, they discovered only six males worldwide that had reproduced by natural means. In 1996, the trend in the world zoo population of pandas indicated that for every potential breeding male there were 1.8 breeding females. The ideal ratio for a breeding population is closer to one-to-one. In addition, Lindburg and his Chinese colleagues determined that many potential breeding males were in poor health. Where they failed to breed due to behavioral problems, the two most prominent causes of failure were hyperaggression and disinterest in females. This important archival study reveals a serious deficiency in the world zoo population. Consequently, Zoo Atlanta's research on panda socialization is primarily concerned with developing males.

When Rebecca Snyder first arrived in China in 1997, she observed pairs of pandas during the spring mating season. When she returned in the fall, she was able to observe mothers and their offspring. One of her subjects produced twins and Snyder was able to gather data on a very rare phenomenon, a mother who attended to both of her offspring. Until this case, experts had concluded that mothers routinely neglect one of the twin offspring, even though twins occur roughly 40 percent of the time in captivity. (We don't know the rate of twinning in nature.) If the propensity of mothers to abandon a twin is a reliable phenomenon, it may occur because of the extremely small

Chengdu Zoo, Zhong Wei

ZOO ATLANTA RESEARCHER REBECCA SNYDER POSES PROUDLY WITH BABY XIAO SHUANG,
ONE OF A PAIR OF TWINS AT THE CHENGDU ZOO.

Chengdu Research Base

ZOO ATLANTA CONSERVATION EDUCATOR SARAH BEXELL, NANYA, AND LUO LAN WITH QI ZHENG
AND LIU JIU IN CHENGDU, DECEMBER 1999.

size of panda offspring. Panda mothers are 800 times larger than their cubs, compared to other bears, which are roughly 280 times bigger. In fact, panda cubs are more helpless than most social carnivores. As a result, panda mothers typically experience a post-partum fast, which can last 25 days or more. During this fasting period, the tiny, nearly hairless baby suckles as many as fourteen times a day and demands the full attention of its mother. For a mother to handle two demanding offspring, supplementary feeding may be essential. Thus, the Chengdu managers gave the mother some assistance after a month of reasonably successful parenting.

Data from China provide some developmental norms for giant pandas. In a study of seven infants at Wolong, infants were all pink in color with a white coat of soft down, known as lanugo, at birth. Black pigmentation and the first signs of body hair were first noted at 7–10 days. Eyes opened at 35–48 days, ears at 31–50 days. Deciduous dentition was first recorded at 82–121 days. The first eruption of permanent teeth occurred at 350 days. For additional information on maternity in pandas see Table 5-2.

Based on Snyder's observations of five mothers and their developing infants at the Chengdu Research Base for Giant Panda Breeding and the Chengdu Zoo, we know that baby pandas receive intensive contact and stimulation from their mothers. This tactile contact through touching, holding, and licking may provide an emotional bridge to independence and a kind of rudimentary "self-esteem." Reticence, disinterest, and even hyperaggressiveness may result from a lack of contact and support early in life. Just as Harlow's isolated and socially deprived monkeys failed to bond with peers, pandas separated too early from their mothers can be harmed. For a number of years it has been standard procedure in Chinese zoos and breeding centers to separate pandas from their mothers at four to six months of age, in order to ensure that the mother can exhibit estrus and become pregnant each year. This decision was a result of efforts to increase the absolute numbers of pandas born. Technical staff who are particularly successful are paid a bonus. We had to put forth a fairly persuasive argument just to gain permission to leave four mothers with their infants for twelve months. Although baby pandas are gaining some measure of independence in their second six months of life, this is a crucial period for psychological development, particularly for males. We believe that twelve months' worth of mothering is far better than six months' worth — but wild pandas are getting mothering

# – TABLE 5-2 –
## MATERNITY IN WILD GIANT PANDAS
(Constructed from data in Zhu, Lindburg, Pan, Forney, and Wang, 2000.)

| | |
|---|---|
| First estrus | 3 years |
| First litter | 6 years |
| Birth signs | Reduced activity 30 days prior to birth |
| Gestation | Mean = 146.3 days |
| Preferred den | Rock caves |
| Leaves birth site | At 13 days |
| Infant crawls | At 2 months |
| Infant walks | At 4.25 months |
| Abandons den | Mean = 114.7 days |
| Eats solid food | 5–6 months |
| Weaning | 8–9 months |
| Independence | 2–3 years |
| Birth interval | 2 years |
| Cubs/lifetime | 7–8 |
| End of breeding | 20 years |

Zoo Atlanta, Megan Wilson

LIU JIU GETS TENDER ATTENTION FROM MOTHER YA YA IN THE OUTDOOR YARD AT CHENGDU RESEARCH BASE FOR GIANT PANDA BREEDING. LIU JIU WAS APPROXIMATELY SIX MONTHS OLD IN THIS PHOTO.

into their second year, so the captive panda is still getting a lesser education in the art of social behavior.

It will take a few years to demonstrate that our approach to panda management is correct. Meanwhile we advise taking a conservative position. Since wild pandas stay with or near their mother for as long as two and one half years, why not leave zoo pandas with their mothers for at least eighteen months? By this standard it is possible to give the mothers a beneficial two-year birth interval. A longer time with its mother shifts the emphasis from quantity to quality of offspring. In my opinion, pandas with at least eighteen months of mothering are better prepared for social life, reproduction, and parenting. By encouraging a normal socialization, giant pandas are free to develop with fewer psychological flaws. The current generation of adult pandas in captivity is tainted by social deprivation. We must act now to improve the performance of future generations.

I believe that our work in zoos must be complemented by intensive fieldwork in China. Two such researchers, Pan Wenshi and Lu Zhi of Peking University, continue to document panda behavior in the wild. This is the proper context to understand data acquired in zoos. For example, Pan and Lu have evidence that pandas may be more sociable in the wild than we thought. It appears that they sometimes form loose associations resembling organized groups. The "solitary" panda also apparently learns from males in the vicinity of its home turf. As Lu Zhi of Peking University found in her study of wild pandas: "Hu Zi, who had spent years learning from his mother, now passed hours watching and following the more experienced male, who roamed the forest as if he owned the place." Familiar pandas may associate more than unfamiliar pandas. A more complex socialization is possible when animals other than the mother interact with offspring. Pandas may not be so solitary after all.

Our multidisciplinary research program, based on field and lab data, should lead to precise management mandates. In this sense we are acting as applied scientists working for the betterment of our clients, the pandas. Soon we will have a blueprint for optimal panda development, and we will seek to arrange it so that all zoo pandas can adopt a naturalistic lifestyle similar to their kin in the protected bamboo forests of China.

Zoo Atlanta, Megan Wilson

YA YA WITH LIU JIU AND WU JIU IN THE OUTDOOR YARD AT THE CHENGDU RESEARCH BASE. ALL THREE PANDAS ARE RESTING ON THEIR WOODEN CLIMBING STRUCTURE.

# VI.
# CARING FOR PANDAS

Caring for the giant panda is partly art and partly science. Dedicated keepers, nutritionists, and veterinarians have devoted their careers to learning the preferences and aversions of pandas. One thing that we have learned about the giant panda is how hazardous it is to generalize. Giant pandas are individuals that differ in their likes and dislikes. At Zoo Atlanta, for example, we have discovered that the young pandas Lun Lun and Yang Yang have distinct preferences for certain species of bamboo, and these preferences change frequently! As this book is written, they seem to prefer *Arundinaria gigantea* (Rivercane), *Pseudosasa japonica* (Arrow), and *Sasa palmata*. There are other species that they will eat seasonally, and some that they sometimes eat—but we are not always sure why they accept the latter. So far, we have tried eighteen species of bamboo with mixed results.

The acquisition of acceptable bamboo has proved to be one of the most difficult problems for panda managers in Atlanta. On a daily basis, panda keepers provide 150–200 pounds of bamboo for the two animals. Each of the Atlanta pandas consumes 20–25 pounds each day, so they do not eat about one third of the food that is placed before them. The bamboo is provided continuously throughout the day, with a large quantity available at night. When it comes to the day-to-day care of giant pandas, the processing of bamboo is our most time-consuming duty. Commissary, horticulture, and panda-house staff must acquire, clean, weigh, bundle, cut, cool, and distribute the bamboo day and night. Because we study the pandas' eating habits, a lot of time is spent evaluating and discussing their response to various foods. We

Zoo Atlanta, SEBO

YANG YANG AND LUN LUN SPEND A COOL MORNING MUNCHING ON BAMBOO IN AN OUTDOOR HABITAT AT ZOO ATLANTA.

require a full-time staff of experts in "bamboo keeping" to supplement the work of the five full-time zookeepers needed to manage the two pandas.

As you can tell, bamboo is almost a mantra at Zoo Atlanta. We might as well be bamboo eaters too, just like the pandas, for as much time as we think and talk about it. Our Commissary leader Gloria Hamor must dream about bamboo. (More likely she has nightmares!) We manage to obtain just enough bamboo for the critters, but it is labor intensive and incredibly challenging for the staff and volunteers who work at this demanding task. Prior to the pandas' arrival, we had identified 14 sites to acquire bamboo. Since their arrival we have identified 317 sites around Atlanta, some of them as far away as 100 miles. Our staff is constantly on the lookout for good bamboo, which must carefully be evaluated when they find it. Fortunately, we get some help from Georgia panda lovers; we get many calls each week from people offering bamboo. In a single day we have employed as many as fifteen people to evaluate, harvest, and prepare bamboo! In the future, it is likely that we will operate our own bamboo farms off-site. We need large parcels of land to grow particular varieties of bamboo. Concerned friends of the zoo have already offered valuable land for this pur-

pose. It appears that we are now firmly entrenched in the bamboo business.

At Zoo Atlanta, we also feed the pandas a commercially available biscuit (Marion Red Leafeater Biscuit) in a diet developed by nutritionists at the San Diego Zoo. This high-fiber food is provided five times per day. The female Lun Lun will eat apples and peanut butter, but Yang Yang is not currently eating other foods. Our keepers have established that each animal dislikes certain foods. Lun Lun dislikes pears, carrots, grapes, raisins, Cheerios, and shredded wheat. Yang Yang does not like carrots, grapes, or honey; as this book goes to press, he has just begun to accept apples. These are all foods that other pandas have eaten, so when it comes to food, pandas can be mighty persnickety. By contrast Blair (1938) reported that Pandora, the first young panda at the Bronx Zoo, consumed with enthusiasm a mixture of milk, egg, honey, pablum, and fish liver. Historically, zoos have fed a more varied diet to pandas, but this is not an acceptable strategy today. When it comes to eating, it is apparent that the giant panda is highly specialized. Because of the high percentage of bamboo in their diet, pandas must consume large quantities to receive sufficient nutrition. In the wild and in the zoo, giant pandas are busy eating most of the time.

THE PANDA HOLDING FACILITY INCLUDES A STATE-OF-THE-ART BAMBOO MISTING ROOM THAT KEEPS SUPPLIES
OF CUT BAMBOO AS FRESH AND CRISP AS POSSIBLE FOR FINICKY EATERS.

Zoo Atlanta, SEBO

KEEPER SPRINA LIU PASSES A "PANDA BISCUIT" TREAT TO LUN LUN.

While the people who care for giant pandas are the most important variables in their daily lives, the quality of their living space is also very important. Zoo Atlanta has a stellar reputation for the quality of its exhibits. Historically, we have designed our exhibits to meet animal, caretaker, and visitor needs. The design firm CLR (principally Jon Coe and Gary Lee) of Philadelphia planned the giant panda exhibit in Atlanta. Holder Company, a highly regarded local construction firm, superbly executed the plan. The pandas were provided 10,656 square feet of usable outdoor habitat, and air-conditioned dayrooms comprised of additional 1,000 square feet. Another 2,118 square feet of tunnels, chutes, halls, dens, and porches have been built. The animals can be easily separated at any time. Altogether, the two pandas have access to more than 13,000 square feet of space. The special features of the Atlanta facilities include indoor-outdoor viewing, temperature/humidity control indoors, weighing scales, privacy yard, climbing structures, bamboo cooler and misting device, audio-video monitoring system with sixteen cameras, squeeze cages, kitchen/office, and an automatic watering system. In a letter supporting our application to receive giant pandas, the Chinese Association of Zoological Gardens concluded: "Compared with other institutions which currently house the giant panda, the equipment in this facility is the most advanced to date."

I have had the opportunity to see many of the giant panda facilities around the world, including many locations in China. One of the largest is the indoor facility at Hong Kong's "Ocean Park" theme park where visitors are moved slowly through the air-conditioned exhibit by a conveyor-belted "people mover." The extensive panda habitat is planted with living trees on a sloped field where the pandas can always be seen. The San Diego Zoo has also developed an outstanding facility for their giant pandas, and we learned a lot from San Diego's experience. We also studied the older facilities at the National Zoo, where the staff had years of experience in managing pandas. I believe that our panda facilities at Zoo Atlanta compare quite favorably to the best in the world.

In my opinion, the very best panda facilities in China are those at the Chengdu Research Base for Giant Panda Breeding, established in 1987. Here both giant pandas and red pandas reside in large outdoor compounds. The entire Chengdu Base is comprised of 35.53 hectares, and the largest enclosures are 16,650 square meters. Walls and sloping dry moats separate the animals from the public. Although visitors are welcome at

Zoo Atlanta, SEBO

A WONDERFUL OVERVIEW OF ONE OF THE OUTDOOR HABITATS IN THE NEW GIANT PANDA EXHIBIT AT ZOO ATLANTA.

the Chengdu Base, this facility does not experience the large crowds that gather in Chinese zoos. For example, the nearby Chengdu Zoo draws 1.5 million visitors annually. The exhibits at the base are heavily planted with native vegetation, and large climbing structures have been provided for the pandas. The indoor facilities are spacious, with metal bars and concrete floors. Large fans that are operated from the public side cool these indoor quarters. Chengdu is an excellent place to photograph pandas, as many of them are housed socially and the animals are playful. While many zoos in China are examples of "hard architecture," the Chengdu Base is a softer, naturalistic facility, like the most advanced Western zoos. Ingenious management has led to many innovations in housing and husbandry at Chengdu. Since 1953 when the first giant panda was exhibited at the Chengdu Zoo, a total of 56 pandas have been born at the Zoo and the Base. The current population of giant pandas at the Zoo and the Base is 28 animals, one fourth of the total captive population in China.

In addition to discussions of exhibit facilities, we are also teaching our Chinese colleagues about environmental enrichment, a Zoo Atlanta field of specialization. In Atlanta we are providing objects such as "boomer balls," puzzle-feeders, and "bamboo-sickles" to encourage activity in our two young pandas. These and other techniques are utilized in Chengdu at the Base and at the Zoo. At Wolong, San Diego Zoo behaviorists Dr. Ron Swaisgood and Dr. Don Lindburg have collaborated with Chinese specialists to extensively test enrichment as a tool for panda management (Swaisgood, et al., in press). Their work has been very successful.

At Wolong, pandas receiving enrichment were much more active in the presence of the test stimuli, and in many cases stereotyped behavior was reduced or eliminated. In the presence of various forms of enrichment, their activity continued at a high rate, indicating that enrichment was a strongly motivating condition in the lives of these animals. In addition, Swaisgood and his associates discovered that older pandas preferred feeding enrichment to object enrichment. In simpler terms, enrichment keeps pandas active. The most encouraging finding has been the enthusiastic acceptance of enrichment among the panda managers in China. In fact, Wolong staff are helping to spread the word. Workshops planned in the next two years by San Diego, Zoo Atlanta, and CBSG (the Conservation Breeding Specialist Group) of IUCN should further contribute to the improvement of giant panda psychological well-being in the zoos of China.

THE OUTDOOR GIANT PANDA HABITAT AT THE NATIONAL ZOO.

Jessie Cohen, National Zoological Park, Smithsonian Institution

# - ENRICHMENT -

In recent years, zoos have sought to formalize their efforts to enhance the environments and the experiences of zoo animals according to scientific management principles. A new field has developed to encompass these enhancements known as "environmental enrichment." Enrichment in this context takes place in the physical and social environment of the zoo, including the management protocols for husbandry (care, feeding, and cleaning). The field is relatively new (see Shepherdson et al., 1998), but it has been influenced by pioneering zoo biologist Heini Hediger (1930, 1966) and psychobiologist Robert M. Yerkes (1925). Essentially, environmental enrichment takes place when zoo personnel introduce objects or make changes to the social setting or husbandry schedule to improve the psychological well-being of the animals. To some degree, enrichment has been a response to aging facilities and a lack of flexibility and stimulus change. Under such inflexible and unchanging conditions, zoo animals are perceived as bored and inactive. Worse, some animals react to restricted living conditions with stereotyped pacing and other abnormal behavior patterns. Animal rights groups have criticized zoos for failing to improve the lives of wild animals in captivity.

The most significant response to what the environmental psychologist Robert Sommer has labeled "hard architecture" is to design and build naturalistic, "soft" architecture. An example of this is the giant panda exhibit at Zoo Atlanta. The exhibit is large, with both outdoor and indoor facilities, softened by living vegetation throughout, and natural surfaces under foot. The animals have many choices and opportunities to explore and play. Soft architecture caters to the natural proclivities of the creature. Pandas need to climb, and they need soft surfaces and materials for eating, sleeping, and manipulating. To supplement our naturalistic living environment, we are providing moveable objects such as "boomer balls" and manipulable puzzle feeders. Pandas get plenty of browse in the form of their huge daily ration of bamboo. They receive a small amount of supplementary food to provide some

# - ENRICHMENT -

variety and additional nutrition, but unlike other bears, they are highly specialized feeders.

Changes in the physical environment often stimulate activity, but new social opportunities are often more powerful motivators. At one time zoos failed to provide appropriate social groupings for the animals. Gorillas, for example, were often housed alone or in pairs. We learned that gorillas require appropriate social groupings in order to flourish and reproduce. Zoo Atlanta houses its lowland gorillas in two large social groupings, one small group, and one "bachelor" male group, each of them representative of gorilla social life in nature. Although giant pandas are thought to be "solitary" in the wild, there is doubtless considerable variation in the number and kind of social contacts on any given day of a giant panda's life. In the zoo, they happily coexist with social partners in pairs or larger social groupings. For many social mammals, new social opportunities generally stimulate an increase in activity and typically facilitate mating. For

this reason, we believe that groups of giant pandas would be superior to pairs in stimulating reproduction.

Zoo Atlanta specializes in the science of environmental enrichment. My own first publication in the area dates to 1979, and Dr. Mollie Bloomsmith and Dr. Debra Forthman have both written about enrichment issues for more than fifteen years. We emphasize the "science" of enrichment because it is important that we document the effects of our environmental enhancements. Reliable techniques whose effects are clearly understood will be spread to other settings. Informal, anecdotal enrichment experiences will be slower to disseminate, and ultimately may be resisted. Carefully designed studies of enrichment are required if the field is to gain respect among scientists and managers. An enrichment science program is an important demonstration of zoo biology's commitment to animal welfare. Zoo Atlanta and San Diego Zoo behavioral scientists have concluded that giant pandas can benefit from environmental enrichment.

My students and I have spent more than two decades evaluating zoo exhibits and collaborating with landscape architects to design innovations in exhibitry. The first step in developing an optimum program for any species is to learn about its life in the wild. This information is hard to obtain for the giant panda. We know where they live in the wild, but we know very little about how they live. And some things that we know still confuse the designer. For example, the giant panda is believed to be a "solitary" animal. But when and how does it become solitary? Must it be solitary in captivity in order to reproduce properly? Managers at the Chapultepec Zoo in Mexico City reasoned that their young pandas preferred a social life, so they defied the advice of their Chinese colleagues and left them together. Mexico City has the most prolific breeding record for pandas outside China. Given these discrepancies, the designer should build with flexibility in mind. Make it possible for pandas to be together or apart. Let the pandas decide.

We know that giant pandas occupy caves within rocks or dead tree cavities when they are about to give birth. So designers must provide protected areas within the zoo exhibit, inside and outside. We also know that mothers sometimes move their offspring to a new cave, so we had best provide more than one denning place. In the den, the new mother is away from the sire. Baby pandas do not show any signs of independence until the fourth month of life, and they may stay with their mothers into a second year. Working in the field, Dr. Lu Zhi discovered that "Jiao Jiao and Hu Zi stayed together two and a half years, about a year longer than most researchers thought was the norm."

The more I read about the giant panda, and the more I observe them myself, the more convinced I am that they are quite intelligent creatures. Our keepers have observed that the pandas quickly learned how to move about within our complicated night quarters and they have adapted to a new language (English) with no difficulty. Adam Stone, Zoo Atlanta's Coordinator of Enrichment and Training, has been similarly impressed with their ability to learn. To test their capacity formally, Lori Tarou, an advanced graduate student in the School of Psychology at Georgia Tech, will be studying their spatial cognitive skills in China and at Zoo Atlanta. Hopefully, we will soon have a better picture of how quickly giant pandas solve problems, but our pilot data already demonstrate that they exhibit spatial memory comparable to other highly evolved mammals. These are the first data to reveal the mind of the panda. It is

Patricia Reyes-Gómez Llata

YING YING, THE CHAPULTEPEC ZOO'S MOST PROLIFIC FEMALE
PANDA, WITH ONE OF HER OFFSPRING, XI HUA, IN AUGUST 1997.

possible that giant pandas harbor intellectual traits that may surprise keen observers such as George Schaller (1993), who wrote:

"The panda has become a specialist; it has chosen security over uncertainty. But by doing so it has lost its need to explore, to be observant, to try something new; it has tied itself to a fate without a horizon."

We have learned that panda problem-solving is not just an ecological issue. In the wild, giant pandas must locate food, but they must also remember the location of rivals (to avoid dangerous fights) and potential mates. While most of their information is olfactory, some is auditory and some is visual. All of these stimuli must be remembered for long periods of time. To successfully feed, fight, and mate, they must "learn to learn," as Harlow (1971) once phrased it. Learning is a developmental phenomenon; cognitive development and social development are closely related constructs. Zoo Atlanta is the first institution to examine these issues in giant pandas. To carry out this research properly, we will need to study many animals from infancy into old age.

The opportunity to study giant panda cognition, heretofore unstudied in this species, leads to questions

Zoo Atlanta, SEBO

LUN LUN IS PARTICIPATING IN A MEMORY STUDY USING FOOD HIDDEN IN CLOSED CONTAINERS.
SHE EXHIBITS A HIGH LEVEL OF INTELLIGENCE.

that I am frequently asked. Why are there so few giant pandas in American zoos? When will there be more to see and to study? The simple answer is that two governments control the export of giant pandas. While China would certainly gain financially from increased exportation, the American government is seeking to avoid the appearance of "commercialization." In addition, it is not prudent to release too much money too fast into conservation programs. We have learned that

conservation dollars are most effective when they can be carefully applied to local projects by the recipients.

Our Fish & Wildlife Service, the regulator of giant panda loans in this country, is understandably cautious in its approach. We don't have sufficient experience with panda projects in China to know if our funds are doing what we intended, and we must be very careful not to produce "demand" for panda exportation. That is why the first two projects, San Diego and Atlanta, are so

Zoo Atlanta, SEBO

LUN LUN TAKES A DRINK FROM ONE OF THREE SHALLOW POOLS THAT GRACE THE OUTDOOR HABITATS.

important. The two organizations, working under the banner of the American Zoo and Aquarium Association, must demonstrate that the AZA panda program is, first and foremost, an effective conservation program. I believe that it will take at least five years to know that our program is working, or to fine-tune it if necessary. Although there are at least a half dozen zoos that have expressed an interest in acquiring the animals, it is likely that the flow of giant pandas to America will continue to be very slow. Under the current circumstances, this is entirely appropriate. Future panda holders must adhere to stringent guidelines from AZA and the U.S. Fish & Wildlife Service. The Chinese government also has requirements for exhibition, including management protocols that must be strictly followed by American institutions. The low numbers of giant pandas does present problems for zoo biologists. For now, the solution to small sample size is to maintain a larger research program in China. Both Zoo Atlanta and the San Diego Zoo are actively engaged in research at the Chengdu and Wolong breeding facilities. Together, Chinese and American scientists are unraveling the mysteries surrounding the giant panda, China's most enigmatic creature.

# VII.
# BECOMING WORTHY
# OF PANDAS

While I was a Rotary Fellow at the University of Stockholm in 1971, an American friend of mine began to write a satirical column for the student newspaper *Gaudeamus*. I had shared with him my latent skills as an illustrator and he asked me to draw cartoons for his column. He chose to write a piece about America's developing relationship with the People's Republic of China. We were both amused by the proposed exchange of wildlife to symbolize the emerging friendship of the two nations. As the whole world was about to learn, the USA would send two musk oxen (Milton and Matilda) to China in exchange for two giant pandas! I couldn't imagine then or now a worse trade for the Chinese. I am sure that this was the very first time that I ever contemplated the value and significance of giant pandas. As an avid student of diplomacy, I was already beginning to see the relationship between international politics and the science of behavior. In the early days of the American/Chinese *détente*, symbols were just as important as words. Little did I know then that pandas would someday loom large in my life and my career.

Twenty-eight years after the arrival of giant pandas at the National Zoo in Washington, D.C., and just months after their last panda passed away, scientists and architects are studying Zoo Atlanta's panda exhibit as they prepare to acquire replacements. But the situation has changed. In 1972, the Chinese government, anxious to make friends in the West, provided giant pandas *gratis* in the form of diplomatic state gifts. This is how giant pandas appeared in Berlin, Moscow, London, Mexico City, and Tokyo. Then and now, giant

TERRY MAPLE'S 1971 CARTOON OF RICHARD NIXON AND HENRY KISSINGER BRINGING MUSK OXEN TO CHINA.

Jessie Cohen, National Zoological Park, Smithsonian Institution

A PANDA AT REST AT THE NATIONAL ZOO.

pandas have been regarded by the Chinese as symbols of friendship and trust. But there is one important difference in the year 2000. Today, the Chinese government loans its pandas to those who qualify as recipients according to the requirements of the Convention on International Trade of Endangered Species (CITES). And now, Zoo Atlanta has become a mentor. We depended on experts at the National Zoo and the San Diego Zoo while we planned our panda program, and now we are eager to share what we have learned on our own. How we became leaders in giant panda research and conservation is an interesting story.

It certainly seemed an unlikely scenario on June 15, 1984, the day of my baptism as director of the dilapidated and controversy-ridden Atlanta Zoo. Rated by the U.S. Humane Society as one of America's "ten worst zoos," it had been spiraling out of control for a long time. Years of neglect, shrinking budgets, and mismanagement had produced an institution that could not meet the minimal standards of membership in the national zoo association (AZA). The newspapers were filled with stories about the sad state of the animal enclosures, and the Atlanta community had simply stopped going to the zoo. I became director in a crisis as deep as any zoo had ever faced. Repairing the zoo's relationship to the community was our first priority. Fortunately, Atlantans rallied to support the zoo and to provide its new director with a mandate for excellence.

From the earliest days of my directorship, I was confident that our zoo could be vastly improved. Indeed, having grown up in San Diego, I believed that Atlanta's citizens ought to have a zoo of comparable quality. In 1984, I saw no reason that we couldn't eventually achieve true greatness. Our zoo simply needed a coherent vision. But at the time, our history and our unique specializations constrained the zoo. We had heavily invested in a narrow collection of reptiles and amphibians. Obviously, I reflected, the zoo could build on its good reputation in herpetology, the study of reptiles. However, I also believed that no zoo with such an imbalance in the collection would be successful. In 1984, 77% of the collection was comprised of reptiles, amphibians, and invertebrates. The zoo director loves them all, but this was the most skewed distribution of animals of any zoo in the entire nation. Clearly, we had to find another specialty to attract public interest and extend our reputation.

A long-standing partnership with the Yerkes Primate Center of Emory University provided the opportunity we needed. The zoo had housed Yerkes animals since 1968, when Atlanta zoo director John Roth formalized a partnership between the two institutions. In June 1984 I completed a stronger transaction with then-Yerkes Director Dr. Fred King to obtain thirteen gorillas and eleven orangutans on loan to the zoo, if we agreed to design and build world-class facilities to house them. The announcement of this new relationship energized the Atlanta community and transformed the zoo. When we opened the exhibit for gorillas in 1988, the new Ford African Rainforest, sponsored by Ford Motor Company, was an instant hit with the public.

The new Zoo Atlanta was designed to create an immersive, naturalistic environment for people and animals. The Ford African Rainforest was especially innovative in that we designed it to present gorillas as a *population* rather than as a pair or even a single group, as most zoos had done. When the exhibit opened, our visitors could see three family groups of gorillas and one solitary male, the famous "Willie B." Years later, Willie B. would take over the group in habitat three and produce five offspring of his own, testimony to the strong foundation of behavior that contributed to our emerging philosophy of scientific management.

In 1984 we envisioned a new kind of zoo. Zoo Atlanta would seek to become the most scientific zoo in the world, networked with major universities and research laboratories, such as Emory University, Georgia Institute of Technology, University of Georgia, and Yerkes Regional Primate Research Center, and infused with world-class scientific and educational talent. Later on we invested in advanced computerization, telecommunications, and distance technology to be certain that we would operate on the cutting edge of science and education. This investment in technology and talent is continuing. Our formal "Distance Learning" programs are second to none in the zoo profession. Currently, we operate our programs in all 159 Georgia counties, many neighboring and distant states, and in Mexico. All of these features of our scientific vision contribute to our effectiveness in conservation. It is a unique niche that we occupy in the zoo world, and our scholarly reputation has made many things possible, including our giant panda conservation program.

Interestingly, with the exception of Dr. Debra Forthman (who observed them briefly at the Los Angeles Zoo), none of my staff had ever worked with giant pandas before we acquired them. However, we

*continued on page 92*

Zoo Atlanta archives

WILLIE B., A MALE WESTERN LOWLAND GORILLA, SPENT 27 YEARS IN ISOLATION AT THE OLD ATLANTA ZOO.

Zoo Atlanta, SEBO

IN 1988, WILLIE B. WAS "SET FREE" TO LIVE A NATURAL LIFE IN THE FORD AFRICAN RAINFOREST AT THE NEWLY RENOVATED ZOO ATLANTA. HE WAS SOON SOCIALIZED AND SIRED FIVE OFFSPRING BEFORE HIS DEATH IN EARLY 2000.

were deep in experts on herps and nonhuman primates. More importantly we had developed a fine reputation in the zoo world for naturalistic exhibitry, ethical management, and for our ability to regularly publish in high-quality scientific journals. Three of our exhibits in the '90s have been honored with AZA "Significant Achievement" awards. Our great ape breeding program is highly regarded worldwide, receiving an AZA award for significant achievement in "great ape management and research." Our breeding success is evident in the production of eleven offspring during the twelve years since the gorilla exhibit was opened, with the biological mothers raising all but one of the offspring. We are also the world's leading zoo in the breeding of drill baboons, one of the most endangered African primates; eight drills have been born at Zoo Atlanta in ten years. Our stellar record in zookeeping and veterinary medicine are additional qualifications for managing rare species such as the giant panda.

We dreamed of giant pandas at a time when our zoo was just emerging from crisis. By 1987, now re-accredited by the American Zoo and Aquarium Association (AZA), we were certainly good enough to qualify for a short-term panda loan. But our window of opportunity would be short-lived. It would take much better qualifications down the road when pandas could only be obtained on long-term loans. In a strange twist of fate, the upgrading of our zoo coincided with the elevated standards promulgated by the U.S. Fish & Wildlife Service, the federal agency charged with enforcing the Endangered Species Act and issuing permits to import endangered wildlife. Apparently, Zoo Atlanta's timing was just about right. Strangely, while we awaited our opportunity to contend for pandas, no other zoo stepped up to challenge our position. It was as if the others were waiting to see if the first institution in line would survive the more demanding permit requirements. Zoo Atlanta would be the first zoo to be approved under the new guidelines. We have reason to be proud of that achievement.

Fulfilling the dream would also require strong support from the Atlanta business community. We would need to build a new state-of-the-art exhibit, and we would need to generate ten million U.S. dollars for conservation in China. This would be no easy task for a not-for-profit zoo just a decade out of city government. In our history we had never raised such an ambitious amount of money. It would take successful corporate friends with deep pockets to prepare us for

*continued on page 98*

Zoo Atlanta, SEBO

LUN LUN PEERS OUT FROM THE "CAVE" IN OUTDOOR HABITAT NUMBER ONE. THIS CAVE ALSO SERVES
AS A PASSAGEWAY TO OUTDOOR HABITAT NUMBER TWO.

# -CONSTRUCTION-

Zoo Atlanta's giant panda exhibit was a big challenge to our staff, but we had plenty of time to plan it given the many twists and turns along the panda journey. We first designed an exhibit in 1986 and actually built it to accommodate the expected short-term loan of pandas. The first exhibit was relatively simple, and it was designed to hold Malayan tapirs after the pandas returned to China. After the demise of short-term loans, neither pandas nor tapirs ever lived in the exhibit. We decided to house other mammals and birds there: Asian cranes, muntjac antelopes, and later Asian small-clawed otters. Due to the changes, it became known as "exhibit du jour," but it has held up quite well.

Ten years later we designed a much larger panda exhibit in the event that the Chinese government requested a giant panda exhibition during the occasion of Atlanta's Centennial Olympic Games. This Olympic exhibit was executed by CLR, Zoo Atlanta's Philadelphia-based designers since 1984. It was estimated in 1996 that the exhibit would cost $5 million to build. In 1999, we dusted off the plan and subjected it to revision and enhancement as the exhibit had to be more amenable to scientific activities, and it required more visitor amenities to control the expected flood of visitors. We carefully studied exhibits in San Diego and Washington, D.C., to flatten the learning curve. The revised plan would take $7 million to build. Once we made the decision to move forward, we had only seven months to build it before the anticipated arrival of the animals. Zoo Atlanta's Deputy Zoo Director Steve Marshall was responsible for managing

# -CONSTRUCTION-

the project with assistance from Bill Cooper, construction and maintenance manager for the zoo. It was a tough assignment. A complex project on a short timeline cannot be accomplished without an experienced and highly qualified contractor. Fortunately, we were able to recruit Holder Construction, the local firm that had successfully built our award-winning Conservation/Education complex, the Action Resource Center.

Since we had so little time and a tight budget, we brought many tasks in-house. Our graphics coordinator, Ric Washington, designed a unique set of colorful graphics for the adjacent visitors' courtyard. We also accomplished the horticulture ourselves, relying on Curator Ed Santos and his zoo team. This process worked well as it is one of the most beautiful and informative exhibits in the nation. The educational technology is easily the most advanced among world zoos. The graphics had to tell the conservation story while describing the unique biology and behavior of the giant panda. Other unique aspects of the exhibit include the sixteen panda-cams that permit us to watch the pandas twenty-four hours a day, seven days a week, wherever they may be in the exhibit, indoors or outdoors. During the hot Atlanta summer, the pandas are housed in air-conditioned indoor units chilled to 62 degrees Fahrenheit. Given the political delays, we actually finished the exhibit in thirteen months, just days before the pandas arrived on November 5, 1999. Upon their arrival, an *AJC* editorial proclaimed: "Their arrival is rightly the crowning accomplishment of Zoo Atlanta's recent renaissance."

Zoo Atlanta, SEBO

THE HORTICULTURE STAFF AND VOLUNTEERS HARD AT WORK PREPARING THE GIANT PANDA EXHIBIT FOR THE IMPENDING ARRIVALS.

Zoo Atlanta, SEBO

VISITORS' PERSPECTIVE OF AN INDOOR DAYROOM IN THE NEW GIANT PANDA EXHIBIT AT ZOO ATLANTA,
WHICH FEATURES SKYLIGHTS, CLIMBING STRUCTURES, AND CLIMATE CONTROL.

the challenge of giant pandas. Fortunately, Georgia corporations rose to the occasion. UPS, Coca-Cola, Holiday Inn (Bass Hotels and Resorts), Delta Air Lines, Home Depot, Turner Foundation, Whitehead Foundation, Campbell Foundation, Callaway Foundation, Murphy Foundation, and Cox Companies all made hefty donations to our cause. Some of these gifts were unprecedented in the zoo's history.

It is unusual for any zoo to take on an ambitious project without some government help. The General Assembly of the State of Georgia was generous in providing the zoo with funds for technology to drive our panda research program. From this contribution we have created a network of sixteen video cameras to see the pandas anywhere in their exhibit. We are using this advanced telecommunications technology to study the pandas and to provide educational materials to schools, other zoos, and our collaborators in China. Soon we will be offering medical teleconferences for our colleagues in Chengdu and the University of Georgia Veterinary School.

We also found support within our federal government. Over several years, Department of the Interior leaders, managers, and scientists helped me to understand the issues concerning the regulation and management of endangered species. They also kept me informed as the giant panda policy was honed and debated by the experts. In turn, I did my best to assist Interior, especially when they were under attack from House Republicans after the 1994 congressional elections. Working with House Speaker New Gingrich, a fellow Georgian and a friend of the zoo, my goal was to protect the Endangered Species Act itself. Twice I addressed congressional committees to urge protection and continuation of the Act. Thankfully, Speaker Gingrich single-handedly prevented some ominous legislation from becoming law, and the Act survives to this day. Although it took a long time to produce a policy for importing giant pandas, our government thoughtfully constructed a document that would genuinely benefit the dwindling giant panda population in China. They concluded, as we did, that limited exhibition could help the panda if it was executed carefully and properly. From the beginning of this new epic in panda conservation, it was also clear that American zoos working in China would have to reckon with the two powerful ministries that controlled panda exportation. I was hopeful that Forestry and Construction would find a way to work cooperatively, and that our trusted collaborators would chart a course leading to a winning outcome for

Zoo Atlanta, SEBO

FORMER SPEAKER OF THE HOUSE NEWT GINGRICH AND THE HONORABLE LI ZHAOXING, AMBASSADOR OF THE PEOPLE'S REPUBLIC OF CHINA, AT THE VIP RECEPTION AT ZOO ATLANTA.

all concerned. As it turned out, friendship, goodwill, and diligence eventually prevailed.

With the educational programs that Zoo Atlanta now provides, a multitude of school-age children can learn about pandas and other exotic fauna. Through the magic of telecommunications, our children are translocated to China, Africa, South America, and the Okefenokee Swamp. They learn firsthand how animals live, and how people around the world are working together to protect wildlife. The inspiring story and powerful image of the giant panda, if used effectively, may be strong enough to save an important piece of the natural world. Atlantans have already submitted to the power of the panda, just as Washingtonians and San Diegans had submitted before. Our devotion to their cause is deep and unwavering. Such is the passion and the promise of the panda.

# VIII.
# TALKING ABOUT PANDAS

From the first moments of my interest in pandas, I found it difficult to talk about them. In the eighties I knew that only the best zoos would be able to exhibit them. Atlanta's zoo would be a longshot for acquiring pandas. Climbing the zoo ladder would require delicate posturing; a headlong rush into contention would be offensive. I chose to maintain a low profile. When critics shut down short-term loans, pandas became the impossible dream. At our regional conference in 1989, I decided to come out of the closet and reveal my intentions. I participated in a panel discussion entitled "To Panda or Not to Panda: Exploitation or Conservation?" I stated then: "What we would like to do in Atlanta is develop a model panda loan that is a win/win situation for all concerned, especially the panda." I thought this could be accomplished with short-term exhibition or long-term breeding loans, but no zoo had worked out the proper formula for success.

What I learned in those early years was that anything said about giant pandas would attract media attention and unwanted criticism. For this reason alone, most zoo directors avoided pandas like the plague. This was an unusual development, since zoo directors had worked themselves into an acquisitive fever just a few years earlier. Having acquired pandas for exhibition, science, and conservation purposes, it is now my personal responsibility to talk about pandas to anyone and everyone who will listen. We talk about giant pandas with enthusiasm and pride. The task of saving pandas is daunting, but we welcome the opportunity and the challenge.

On November 5, 1999, the first day of pandamonium

# Home Sweet Panda Home

## ZOO ATLANTA'S PANDA HABITAT

**Zoo Atlanta's $7 million, indoor-outdoor panda habitat,** the most sophisticated in the world, opens Saturday. The habitat includes public viewing areas, as well as private places where Yang Yang and Lun Lun can go when they're in the mood for solitude.

LEVETTE BAGWELL / Staff

LOUIE FAVORIT

**The pandas' indoor habitat** is part of the zoo's Wolong Panda Research Station and Management Center. Visitors can see into a dayroom.

**Outdoors, the pandas** have a climbing structure like one they us their native China. Part of the outdoor habitat will afford close-up v

### METRO ATLANTA

Map area

Grant Park

Memorial Dr.

Turner Field

Zoo Atlanta

### HABITAT OVERVIEW

### KEY

1. China Wall entrance/lineu
2. Pandamonium gift shop
3. Air-conditioned day roon with indoor viewing areas
4. Wolong Panda Research and Management Center
5. Outdoor habitat 1: Climb structure here replicates th in their former Chinese hab
6. Outdoor habitat 2: Poter will allow visitors to get wit eight feet
7. Private outdoor habitat: allow for pandas' privacy

---

ON THE ROAD

# A City in Full: V

---

SUNDAY, NOVEMBER 21, 1999

世界日報

星期日 二十一日

## 六千人遊先睹爲快　慵懶見客倫

銷暢品禮　愛人見人寶國州神・滾滾鬧熱　獅舞龍舞

---

# The Washi

FRIDAY, NOVEMBI

## Coos and Concerns For Giant Pandas

### 2 Zoos Revel in Arrivals As Conservationists Worry

**By D'VERA COHN**
*Washington Post Staff Writer*

ATLANTA—She chewed his ear, trying to wake him up. He batted her with his paw. She broke away and scratched herself with her hind leg. He sat up, yawned—and toppled over to snooze some more.

Adorable even when they sleep, two new giant pandas are a sensation at Zoo Atlanta, which is paying China $10 million over the next decade to exhibit them. When Lun Lun (she) and Yang Yang (he) arrived three weeks ago, they were greeted at the airport by an applauding crowd and escorted to their designer habitat by police motorcade. The governor stopped by to visit, and one couple drove several hundred miles to see them for a few hours at a party for $1,000 donors. The fuzzy black-and-white pair went on public

Zoo Atlanta's pandas Yan

display last weekend, an much as tripled since the

"We're a small zoo, bu the giant panda is the big director Terry L. Maple cility once so shabby tha in the early 1980s.

*See* **PANDAS,** A20, Col.

## rable, Impatient Atlanta

By R. W. APPLE Jr.

ATLANTA — This is a city without a historic core, a city in constant evolution — a Deep South version, you might say, of Los Angeles.

It has a past, of course, a real one as well as the one that Margaret Mitchell so vividly imagined in "Gone With the Wind." A decisive Civil War battle was fought over this ground, and the momentous civil rights movement of the 1960's had its principal headquarters here. That most American of products, Coca-Cola, was invented here.

But Atlanta, a city in a hurry, keeps putting its past behind it. If not for the Cyclorama depicting the fighting of 1864 and the superlative Atlanta History Center, with its evocations of Henry W. Grady, the great newspaper editor, and Bobby Jones, the golfer, and, yes, William Tecumseh Sherman, who burned the

pleased to promote itself as "The World's Next Great City" and not another tradition-bound vestige of the Old South.

"Atlanta had never been a true Old Southern city like Savannah or Charleston or Richmond, where wealth had originated with the land," Tom Wolfe wrote in his novel "A Man in Full" in 1998. "Atlanta was an offspring of the railroad business. It had been created from scratch barely 150 years ago, and people had been making money there on the hustle ever since."

**What to do, Page 45.**

Quite so. Atlanta, or rather the Atlanta region, is one of the global capitals of New Money, much of it made in real estate. It goes to build the trophy houses in the ritzy residential area along West Pace's Ferry Road in Buckhead, near the History Center, and to buy the BMW's and Land Rovers that clog the parking lots around Buckhead's many shopping centers and to pay for the fine food and drink in the neighborhood's

Continued on Page 45

## on Post

# 耗資七百萬　熊貓新居

## 16部攝影機\24小時觀察　代化堪稱世界之最備

七音波的司公運貨（UPS）達比優條
裡籠箱大在鬆把正員人作工鳥圖。場
（社聯美）

物園現在是向雅典城喬治...
了讓大熊貓吃到新鮮的竹...
的食物中...
子葉二十一...
內，亞特蘭大動物園將與...
希望對熊貓的行為作研究能...
超過出...

命了「華華」，才以她的名字的最好一個字重新是爬樹，她是爬樹命名為「倫倫」。倫倫在白天最喜歡的遊戲就行家。倫倫在四個半月時，就興母親分開，但她還是與其他的熊貓一起生活。

公熊貓「洋洋」
生日：一九九七年九月八日，體重：一百六十磅，乳名：「洋洋」的乳名是「九九」後來因為有三個荷蘭的機構認養「九九」才以這三個機構的名稱重新命名為「洋洋」。

大熊貓

他的母親共同生活了十三個月熊貓每天要吃掉四十磅的

給成精米喝了準都便開始...
奶。楊米...
玉米...

## A Study in Pandas

"I'm continuing my research because of what we've found," says Megan Reinertsen, who earned her master's degree in behavioral psychology by studying flamingos at Zoo Atlanta.

It'll be love at first look when Lun Lun and Yang Yang, the giant pandas from China, arrive at Zoo Atlanta later this month. Theirs will be household names—and their exhibit lines long and laced with anticipation. While the pandas will be a huge attraction, Zoo Atlanta has another, more important, mission.

Behavioral psychologists Dr. Terry Maple, Rebecca Snyder, and Megan Reinertsen will direct a 10-year project, which enabled the loan from the Research Base of Giant Panda Breeding in Chengdu. They will observe and study the panda pair to help conserve the vanishing species.

"The pandas are not being brought over just for people to look at," says Rebecca, a Georgia Tech doctoral candidate who has already spent 21 months studying pandas at facilities in the Sichuan province.

"In fact, according to the U.S.

*The giant pandas coming to Zoo Atlanta aren't just for show; behavioral psychologists will study the pair for 10 years.*

**THE PANDA PAIR**
**The study:** Differences in behavioral development of the two animals—one raised longer by the mother than the other; changes in sociability as they mature; nutrition data

**Sample behavior to observe:** Playfulness

**Duration of study:** Five years with option to extend loan for an additional five

# The pandas are going to be one of those great moments in our history.

Dr. Terry Maple

top things like Willie B (the celebrity gorilla) going outside after 27 years, or his first offspring, but the pandas are going to be one of those great moments in our history. And I'm hoping there will be many more moments." *Carolanne Griffith Roberts*

in Atlanta, we were immersed in an adoring community and elated by an overwhelming media response. Newspapers around the world told the story of the pandas' exciting arrival on the UPS Panda Express. The panda exhibit at the zoo opened on November 20, and media impressions in November 1999 rocketed to nearly *two billion*, more than 40 times the 1998 figure. Zoo Atlanta's Web site had more than 1.5 million hits in the same period. Every key player in the panda program was the target of radio, television, or print reporters. From the panda keepers to the director, the entire world wanted to talk to us. We awakened with the early birds on the morning shows, and we said goodnight on the late evening news. It was downright exhilarating, but not unexpected. We were aware that every zoo exhibiting giant pandas had experienced record crowds and unprecedented interest. Just a few years back, the birth of a panda in Mexico City elicited 270,000 letters in a contest to name the baby.

In the midst of our euphoric reception, we were caught by surprise when rumors surfaced that key staff at the U.S. Fish & Wildlife Service weren't happy with the animated pandas that appeared in our sponsors' television commercials. We didn't hear about it directly, but the zoo "grapevine" passed it on soon after the words were uttered in a private meeting.

THE GIANT PANDA EXHIBIT OPENED OFFICIALLY WITH THE CUTTING OF THE GARLAND BY LIU SHANGHUA, PRESIDENT – CHINESE ASSOCIATION OF ZOOLOGICAL GARDENS; WU PING GUO, VICE MAYOR OF CHENGDU MUNICIPAL GOVERNMENT; WU ZURONG, COUNSEL GENERAL – THE PEOPLE'S REPUBLIC OF CHINA; JOHN LEWIS – UNITED STATES CONGRESSMAN; DR. TERRY MAPLE; TERRY GORDON – ZOO ATLANTA BOARD OF DIRECTORS; ATLANTA MAYOR BILL CAMPBELL; AND ATLANTA CITY COUNCILMAN JIM MADDOX.

Zoo Atlanta, SEBO

Animating the pandas, our moles explained, trivialized the pandas and the commercial context bordered on "exploitation." I decided to call Washington and bring up the subject myself, however obliquely. The ads were a reasonable *quid pro quo* in view of the size of the corporate gifts, I asserted. Why shouldn't our marketing partners get some credit for bringing the pandas to Atlanta? In fact, they were wonderful commercials. But I clearly understood that the Service would be much happier with us if the "fun" was balanced with more serious content. They wanted our sponsors to use their marketing savvy to directly promote conservation. A meeting in Atlanta was the only way to confront the problem and settle the issue.

As only zoo folk can do, we planned a first-class "wild dog and zebra show" that documented our approach to public relations and marketing. My goal was to address the commercialization issue head-on. We prepared print and video versions of our ads and promotions, and our media and corporate partners were present to respond to questions. We were pleased that the local and national media were covering the scientific side of the panda loan like never before, so I asked our marketing director, Gail Eaton, to document our success in selling the science rather than the sizzle.

We were already placing many stories that explained our studies of panda behavior, and how they contributed to conservation. I was particularly pleased with the news coverage that highlighted my affiliation with the School of Psychology at Georgia Tech. Graduate students such as Rebecca Snyder would soon receive doctoral degrees for their research in comparative psychology conducted at the zoo. The appearance of two gorgeous pandas on the cover of the Georgia Tech alumni magazine reached thousands of alumni and friends of the Institute, and the story greatly enhanced the zoo's credibility as a scientific institution. When Fish & Wildlife Service leaders examined our public relations history, they were visibly impressed. In fact, they encouraged us to share our ideas with the whole zoo industry as a model marketing program for endangered species. Our approach was clearly working on many levels, but the Service was also on the right track. The conservation story requires a big stage, and our corporate sponsors can surely help us to craft a more effective message to reach a larger, global audience.

When you market an endangered species, you carefully walk a tightrope. A credible zoo deploys uplifting messages that dignify the animal, but there

*continued on page 110*

Zoo Atlanta, SEBO

CHINESE DANCE TROUPE PERFORMING AT THE GRAND OPENING OF THE GIANT PANDA EXHIBIT
AT ZOO ATLANTA ON NOVEMBER 20, 1999.

are times when you also want to bring the icon down to the level of humanity — for example, by using a cartoon figure to interest children. We learned this firsthand when we labeled zoo products with a Mike Luckovich cartoon of the revered gorilla Willie B. We applied the cartoon image to coffee cups and T-shirts. It was a wonderful caricature of him. Soon thereafter, I received a few letters from longtime supporters who were offended by the cartoon, which they regarded as demeaning. People often disagree about a playful image. What is demeaning to one is funny to another. I believe you can play with a dignified image if you are credible, but you can't take it too far. In Europe, where they take their zoos seriously, there is no reluctance to represent zoo animals as cartoon figures. Much of the advertising for European zoos is animated. Frankly, I like seeing the zoo in an editorial cartoon, as it puts us in the spotlight. Since we enjoy vast public support in Atlanta, such cartoons are generally friendly, and Mr. Luckovich has a unique gift for enlarging the image of zoo critters and zoo directors. (Luckovich was the first artist to discover that Willie B. and I occupied the same amount of space.)

Cartoons can be very effective in advertising, and we were pleased when The Coca-Cola Company decided to create their animated panda advertisement. In fact, we asked them to do it, in part because we liked their polar bear ads. (I am still hopeful that Coca-Cola will someday help me build the world's finest and "coolest" polar bear exhibit at the zoo.) When it comes to the Coca-Cola polar bears, anthropomorphism (humanizing animals) seems to work. When I felt comfortable with the likelihood that we would get pandas from China, I approached my friends at Coke to pitch the sponsorship. In a roomful of experienced marketeers, Gail Eaton, Rebecca Snyder, and I extolled the powerful image of pandas and the importance of our conservation work in China. We believed that a panda image would be easily the equal of a polar bear on television. We urged the company to develop a market-based sponsorship that would simultaneously generate sponsorship dollars for conservation and captivate the public. The finished piece was wonderful, and it debuted on the day the pandas arrived in Atlanta. UPS also used animation to promote the pandas.

In the Coke ad a group of pandas gathered to view a new baby, toasting the occasion with a collective sip of the product. Of course, the Coca-Cola pandas are not real live bears. Animated bears can be humanized;

they can sip Coke, stand upright, or wink at the audience. Animation allows us to separate the "sales bear" from the living bear. In an ideal world, the Coca-Cola panda bears would simultaneously promote a soft drink and conservation. For our part, Zoo Atlanta will continue to search for creative ways to engage, educate, and encourage the public.

We had a short window to market in 1999, but the combined impact of the bears and the media was electric. Our creative work in partnership with the Cox media companies — newspaper, radio, television, and online — was ubiquitous in the marketplace. The entire panda campaign, directed by Gail Eaton, created by Ogilvy & Mather, was so successful that the zoo was honored with the prestigious MAX Award presented by Georgia State University's College of Business Administration and the *Atlanta Business Chronicle* for excellence in marketing. The panelists who judged the nominees were impressed by the decade-long process that enabled Zoo Atlanta to become one of only two zoos in the United States to feature pandas. The ability to combine a marketing objective with the goal of conserving an endangered species was also impressive, according to the judges. Locally, we have succeeded in our efforts to market conservation, but the panda story

had even longer legs. As 1999 came to a close, *The New York Times* named Zoo Atlanta as one of its ten year-end "winners" for the Southeast.

As we have seen, pandas are twentieth-century animals. As advertising became more sophisticated and technology encouraged more powerful imagery, pandas and other wildlife symbols were more frequently utilized in commerce. The jaguar became a symbol of automotive elegance, tires were as tough as rhino hide, a tank of gas created the equivalent of tiger power. But I don't think we've gone far enough in the use of wildlife symbols.

Sports teams long ago discovered animals as mascots and logos, but they haven't been very creative about it. At the college level there are far too many bulldogs, cougars, eagles, and wildcats. The pros are just as unimaginative: jaguars, tigers, lions, and panthers come to mind. There are some animals that have never been selected for nicknames — for example, nearly all of the otherwise popular monkeys and apes (with the notable exception of the Pittsburg [Kansas] State Gorillas!). I'd like to see more creative alliteration with a wider variety of animals. How about the Minnesota Macaques, Washington Warthogs, or Chattanooga Chimpanzees?

The tide is turning a bit with the NHL debut of Ted Turner's Atlanta Thrashers, named for the Georgia state bird. Zoo Atlanta has enjoyed a marketing partnership with the Thrashers, and we depict the genuine bird on zoo graphics. But zoo directors will really pay attention when a percentage of the sporting gate supports a relevant wildlife cause or the recovery of an endangered namesake. Stepping in the right direction, the Baltimore Orioles recently sponsored a wildlife night for the U.S. Fish & Wildlife Service. As sports marketing techniques are applied to conservation, more people will take notice. After all, wildlife conservation is frequently as much about people as it is about animals. As we must convert a planet's worth of people to the cause of conservation, we had best use the most proven marketing techniques to get the job done.

# IX.
# SAVING THE GIANT PANDA

What will it take to save the giant panda from extinction? Clearly, there is a need for better and more continuous information about panda populations. It has been more than a decade since we obtained an objective estimate of their numbers in the wild. It would seem unlikely that their numbers have increased beyond the estimated 1,000 or so animals remaining wild in China. But how far have their numbers declined? Unfortunately, no one really knows. As we enter the twenty-first century, I can think of no higher priority than to conduct an accurate giant panda census. Once we know how many of them remain in nature, we can better evaluate and rank our options for conservation.

As giant pandas are found only in small pockets of dense forest in the mountains of southwestern China, north and central portions of Sichuan province, the most southern regions of Gansu, and in the Qin Ling Mountains of Shaanxi province, they are isolated and at great risk of extinction. Their range was once much larger, extending throughout southern China and into Myanmar. In the past twenty years, panda habitat has been reduced by 50 percent, with only six forest fragments remaining. Inbreeding may damage isolated populations of pandas, since they cannot locate suitably distant mates. Habitat destruction continues to be the greatest threat to giant panda survival in the wild. China's one billion human inhabitants compete with pandas for land and natural resources. Nearly the whole of China is under some form of cultivation or development. Given these pressures, the central government of China has acted to set aside some 28 nature

Zoo Atlanta, SEBO

YANG YANG AND LUN LUN ARE FED OVER 200 POUNDS OF FRESH BAMBOO EACH DAY.

preserves where bamboo supports populations of giant pandas. A recent plan, developed in cooperation with the World Wildlife Fund, would add additional reserves and seventeen connecting migration corridors.

The Chinese government has also provided severe penalties for people convicted of poaching giant pandas, at one time a serious problem within China. Even today a visitor will sometimes discover a fur artifact allegedly made from giant pandas. Sadly, the panda's endearing appearance does not protect them from hard-hearted poachers with short-term profits as their motivation. Sadder still, there are individuals throughout the world who are eager to acquire the skin and fur of endangered animals senselessly slaughtered by poachers. Pelts still sell in the Far East for more than $10,000. In the Qin Ling Mountains, six pandas have been lost to poachers in recent years.

Even though we are uncertain about the size of the giant panda population, we must still make intelligent decisions that will have a positive impact on them. Without the baseline estimate, however, it is difficult to know if our conservation efforts are working. Whatever we choose to do, we have to be careful to do no further harm. We do know that the nation of China harbors a unique population of wildlife. There are more than 500 species of mammals in China, and more than 1200 species of birds. Even more impressive is the fact that China contains 12 percent of the entire world's known species of fish. China also harbors many species "endemic" to China, species that are found *only* in China, such as the giant panda.

Monitoring giant panda populations on a daily basis serves another purpose: field biologists provide their eyes and their ears to record and deter poaching and illegal deforestation. The mere presence of field biologists helps to protect the animals they study. Therefore, when we invest in scientific programs conducted in the field, there are also tangible conservation benefits. One of the best gifts to giant pandas and other endangered wildlife would be significant increases in the budgets of government agencies, foundations, societies, and other nongovernmental organizations that support wildlife conservation and field biology. In this sense, conservation is really all about people. We simply need more people to become involved in scientific conservation. While there is much that outside scientists can do, it is far healthier to create wellsprings for conservation and science in the host countries where the wildlife are at risk. As we have seen, there are encouraging trends in China where young biologists are eager to play a role. A superior investment of conservation dollars is the provision of training and support for an army of dedicated conservation biologists.

At work in China since 1980, the World Wildlife Fund has made training conservation personnel one of its top priorities. Starting in Sichuan province, one of the largest panda reserves, WWF funding built and equipped a research laboratory and captive-breeding center near the Wolong Nature Reserve headquarters from designs contributed by curators at the Wildlife Conservation Society. At this and other sites in China, WWF works to evaluate how infrastructure contributes to panda conservation. Hopefully, infrastructure improves staff motivation and leadership, and contributes to building conservation awareness in the workforce and the surrounding community. In 1998, as a result of a growing consensus on conservation, the Sichuan provincial government banned logging in all natural forests. As this book is written, WWF is working with the Chinese State Ministry of Forestry on the third giant panda census. Early data indicate that the population is stable, and that earlier estimates (1985–88 census) may have undercounted the population. We can only hope that this proves true. The new census is expected to take five years to complete.

Counts will be aided by a high-tech global positioning system that integrates satellite imagery and field surveys on the ground.

A conservation army will not be created without inspiration. For this reason we must continue to engage in a vigorous public awareness campaign. In the zoo world, we accomplish this through conservation education programs, both formal and informal. We must actively teach about wildlife and the ecosystems in which they live. And through this active public education, we must also inspire young people to contribute some of their time and resources to the cause of conservation. Some of the inspired will devote their careers to wildlife, others will support conservation programs through contributions, advocacy, or by their support of conservation-minded public officials.

Beyond its important fieldwork, the World Wildlife Fund has been a pillar of strength in building awareness about conservation. Since its adoption as the WWF logo, the image of the giant panda has become the very symbol of global conservation. This did not happen by accident. In 1961, cofounder Sir Peter Scott selected the giant panda as an instantly recognizable and easily reproducible image for the organization, its unique coloration being a godsend of

*continued on page 121*

Zoo Atlanta, SEBO

A ZOO ATLANTA DOCENT USES A MODEL OF A GIANT PANDA SKULL TO EXPLAIN THE DIFFERENCES BETWEEN PANDAS AND OTHER BEARS.

Jessie Cohen, National Zoological Park, Smithsonian Institution

A GIANT PANDA AT THE NATIONAL ZOO PLAYS IN THE SNOW.

graphic simplicity and familiarity. The giant panda's unique potential to inspire conservation is best represented in the words of George Schaller:

"Having transcended its mountain home to become a citizen of the world, the panda is a symbolic creature that represents our efforts to protect the environment. . . . It has been patterned with such creative flourish, such artistic perfection, that it almost seems to have evolved for this higher purpose."

The giant panda's compelling image has shaped public opinion before. After the famous panda Su Lin arrived at Chicago's Brookfield Zoo in the mid-thirties, her face appeared in newspapers throughout the country. Prior to her capture, Americans knew pandas only by the pelts acquired for museums by hired guns. Page (1984) observed that Su Lin's "cuddly presence" quickly remade public opinion:

"People were outraged that anyone ever again would deliberately shoot such an adorable creature. The four Americans who had shot giant pandas vowed they would never again do such a thing."

In 1980 the American Zoo and Aquarium Association voted to assign conservation as the first priority of its members. But wildlife conservation is never simple to implement, and zoos have come to differ on how they carry out the conservation priority. I like to think of conservation as holistic, comprised of science, education, advocacy, and action. A comprehensive approach to conservation would require that zoos contribute their time and resources equally, but few of us have the expertise or ability to do so. Therefore, zoos tend to specialize and to focus. Larger institutions, such as the Wildlife Conservation Society (WCS) of New York, contribute enormous sums of money to carry out *in situ* ("on-site") conservation throughout the world. WCS is uniquely qualified to function as a worldwide leader in conservation. They operate 320 conservation programs in 52 countries. WCS scientists such as George Schaller are highly visible and enormously productive.

Other zoos have elected to provide financial resources to fund *in situ* conservation, or they have applied their resources locally to build conservation awareness and inspire action. One of the AZA zoos that is currently active in China is the Columbus (Ohio) Zoo. Columbus exhibited pandas on short-term loan in 1992. They were the last AZA zoo to do so prior to the moratorium on short-term loans. A large portion of the revenues associated with the giant panda exhibition in Columbus was released to a foundation endowment that continues to provide funds for conservation projects in China, including projects that are essentially educational. The conservation education model is essential as it offers opportunities for local people to participate in conservation. As important as it is in America, it is critical to provide conservation education in nations where *in situ* conservation has established roots. To this end, both WCS and Zoo Atlanta have initiated conservation education programs in China.

In 1993, WCS became the first Western nongovernmental organization outside China to bring environmental education into China's schools. In China, science is revered and students enthusiastically enter all scientific disciplines. WCS scientist-educators persuaded Chinese administrators to expand their definition of science to include the multidisciplinary field of "environmental studies." For example, in Yunnan province, WCS found willing partners in the local educational establishment, the Kunming Institute of Zoology, and the Kunming Zoo. Utilizing WCS curricula, translated into Chinese, teachers were

trained and programs were developed for school-age children in a variety of settings. As Annette Berkovitz, the WCS executive who developed the program, recently explained:

"This unique collaboration exploits the strengths of each partner to bring new environmental consciousness to the millions of students who will direct their nation's future."

Inspired by these efforts and her successful experience as an educational mentor in Chengdu, Sichuan province, Zoo Atlanta's conservation educator Sarah Bexell initiated a similar program that utilizes the giant panda as a model for conservation education. Combining visits to the Chengdu Zoo and the Chengdu Research Base for Giant Panda Breeding, the program will enable students to learn about panda biology and behavior, and the environmental challenges that must be overcome if giant pandas and other living creatures are to survive in China. It is Sarah's belief that pre-kindergarten-age children may be the keys to conservation commitments by future generations. To quote R. A. Wilson (1996):

*continued on page 125*

STUDENTS AT A CHENGDU KINDERGARTEN PARTICIPATE IN CONSERVATION EDUCATION PROGRAMS.

Sarah Bexell, Zoo Atlanta

YANG YANG ADOPTS A RELAXED POSE FOR THE CAMERA.

Zoo Atlanta, SEBO

"Unless children develop a sense of respect and caring for the natural environment during their early years, they are at risk of never developing such attitudes later in life."

Our newest opportunity in conservation education is the use of advanced telecommunications technology. People interested in giant pandas can use the Internet to gather and exchange information that is often instantaneous. "Panda-Cams" at the San Diego Zoo and at Zoo Atlanta enable the Web surfer to observe pandas in real time. When Hua Mei was born at the San Diego Zoo in August 1999, it was possible just days after her birth to view video footage including vocalizations. The Zoo Atlanta Web site (www.zooatlanta.org) is also linked to other Web sites, including the World Wildlife Fund (www.worldwildlife.org) and the U.S. Fish & Wildlife Service (www.fws.gov). The Internet has a vast number of panda sites where information can be obtained. In Atlanta we are using our distance learning network to provide panda video and information to public schools in the state of Georgia and elsewhere throughout the nation. An AZA educational program for zoos supporting the Giant Panda Foundation will be the next telecommunications project that we will share with our partners.

As China opens up to the outside world, young people from different backgrounds, with active minds and unprecedented technical expertise, are collaborating to create a better world. Today's conservation community compares notes on the Internet and exchanges ideas in a teleconference. It is relatively easy to monitor *in situ* conservation given the speed of today's jet aircraft. Just as easily, we communicate through experienced translators who are equally facile in English and Chinese. A consensus about conservation in China grows more likely with each passing day.

The first step in the scientific method is observation. Conservation too starts with observation. We must keep our eyes on the giant panda. We must observe them to learn more about them. We must watch them to keep them safe from poachers. We must carefully monitor their habitat to preserve the resources they need to live. We must remain eternally attentive, objective, vigilant. Clearly, it will take the best efforts of a knowledgeable and caring citizenry to bring about fundamental environmental change in China. In the case of the giant panda and of so many species throughout the world, love is not enough. Hopefully, love and appreciation for wildlife will motivate a virtual planet of people who must think, work, and act on behalf of all the world's creatures, great and small. If we can truly make the giant panda secure in the wilds of China, we will be successful elsewhere. In this way, the giant panda is a kind of "Holy Grail" of conservation; it is the veritable standard of what we have learned, and what we are willing to endure to stay the course. But given the ups and downs of panda conservation, is it truly a worthy symbol for conservation itself? As conservation is always complex and never easy, universally political and expensive, and by its nature always local, our experience in saving pandas is not atypical. Frankly, we must endeavor to ensure that it becomes a winning symbol. As the Chinese say, a journey of a thousand miles begins with a single step. Saving pandas is a long, arduous journey. We have already taken the first steps.

Zoo Atlanta, SEBO

YANG YANG SHOWS HIS CURIOSITY ON HIS FIRST DAY OUTDOORS AT ZOO ATLANTA.

# EPILOGUE:
# THE EXTENDED PANDA FAMILY

Imagine the giant panda as kin. They are, after all, "mammalkind," just like you and me. Of course, once you have been introduced to a giant panda, you will likely experience feelings reserved only for kin. The panda's power to trigger affection is 100 percent reliable. But will love motivate us to act on their behalf? This is the great challenge for all conservation organizations. How do we inspire people to engage in effective conservation action? On behalf of giant pandas and other living creatures, how do we get the attention of decision-makers? How do we advance the conservation agenda? And the friendly zoogoer . . . what can he or she do to help?

George Schaller's (1993) insightful book on giant pandas and panda politics included valuable advice about how to encourage conservation in field settings.

He observed that conservation cannot be imposed, that it must involve local people based on their interests, skills, and traditions, and it must provide both spiritual and economic benefits.

We are learning that there is indeed spiritual value in conservation. By tending the earth and its resources, we commune with the natural world in a traditional, timeless fashion. The spiritual connection to conservation, for religious people, is doubtless more enduring than economic incentives. Leaders at the Minnesota Zoo surely acknowledged spirituality when they crafted the motto for their mission statement: "Strengthening the bond between people and the living earth." This, I believe, is the most powerful motto in the entire zoo world. The words resonate with feeling; they also encourage people to act. With their own marketing savvy and help from established marketing gurus, modern zoos are rather good at promoting conservation on both emotional and intellectual levels.

Progressive zoos also specialize in providing opportunities for people to help wildlife. The first step is to join with others who support conservation. In Atlanta, we invite our zoo visitors to join our support group, "Friends of Zoo Atlanta." Zoo members receive a colorful quarterly magazine with information about wildlife, where they learn what programs the zoo is supporting in the field, at the zoo, and in the school system. We provide our members (now numbering more than 50,000 households) with plentiful opportunities to learn and to act. They may also become more actively engaged as volunteers, travel with us on conservation-oriented ecotours, or help to educate our visitors in their role as specially trained docents (www.zooatlanta.org). We also urge our members to join with other organizational partners (e.g., WWF, WCS, or the Nature Conservancy) who share our conservation vision. More than seven million members of AZA support organizations nationwide receive regular information about wildlife from their local zoos or aquariums.

One of the best characteristics of zoo support groups is their commitment to optimism. Doomsday conservation messages just don't work anymore, if they ever did. In fact, research has demonstrated that scare tactics are not effective devices in teaching or in motivating recipients. Far better, I think, to give your supporters reason to hope. And there is good reason to hope and to participate. In an important essay, Erik Beever (2000) wrote:

" . . . an overly skeptical perspective may result in missed opportunities to create revolutionary ideas, develop new methods, or formulate new questions."

Beever added that if we failed to give rational people reason for hope, we might generate resistance to conservation biology and a negative perception of its practitioners. Obviously, there is much at stake in our efforts to win support for our common cause. There are right and wrong ways to promote conservation. We must introduce our supporters to our many programs that are succeeding in the field. We cannot ignore impending doom, but we shouldn't wallow in it either.

Ten years ago I discovered a discipline known as "social marketing." In a widely influential textbook, Kotler and Roberto (1989) provided details about marketing a cause. Essentially, the principles of marketing psychology can be deployed in the zoo marketplace. To induce or change behavior, we must first establish a baseline. What do people think about wildlife conservation now? If we find that only 10 percent of our visitors know how few giant pandas remain in the wild, then we must labor to improve their understanding. Once awareness has advanced, then we can try to move them to engage in some significant action on behalf of the cause. Many zoos have focused on letter-writing campaigns to register their concerns. The basics of traditional marketing have been used to promote national political candidates and local bond issues. In business, these same principles sold soap, automobiles, and real estate. Used properly, social marketing can help us to establish a strong base of support for conservation. In America, we can promote a national fundraising campaign to support fieldwork; in China, a concerned nongovernmental organization might someday rally public disdain against local poachers using street theater or billboards.

We have also learned that corporations, media, and the cause are easy alliances to manage when all sides share a common conservation vision. In Atlanta we brought together sponsoring corporations to under-write the cost of television programs that informed the viewer and promoted conservation. For its part, the station provided expertise and loaned broadcast time and talent to create and produce the programs. Corporations headquartered in Atlanta have provided gratis air transportation, rooms and board, and other necessities to facilitate film production. We see these corporations as our partners in conservation. With the help of our local and global media (such as WSB-TV and CNN), we have tried to keep conservation alive on television. During the past decade, I doubt that any zoo in this country has received more favorable and compelling media coverage.

Like many conservation organizations, Zoo Atlanta is a provider of conservation curriculum, materials, and programs based on sound science. We offer many of these programs free of charge to our public schools through "distance learning" on the "Georgia Statewide Academic and Medical System" (GSAMS). Through this fiber-optic, two-way television network, we tell wildlife stories that can be reinforced in family discussions at home. So what should you tell your children when you finish a visit to the zoo? First, I recommend that you tell them that we *can* save the animals if we all do the right things for a long time. We will have to find a way to save wildlife habitat, and we must solve the problem of wildlife poaching. These problems will be especially challenging in China. And remember, optimism works, while pessimism only discourages and defeats children. Kids worry about wildlife, and they depend on adults for the uplifting messages that give them hope for a better future. If we inspire them, our children will do the right thing when they alone are responsible for protecting the environment.

The giant panda story is being played out in real time, and panda conservation will surely require a measure of eternal vigilance. Zoo educators teach children that "extinction is forever." The meaning of this phrase is that after extinction, no human being will ever again see a living representative of the species. Children understand that endangered wildlife can only be saved by people. At the zoo, children tell us that they want to help save giant pandas and other endangered species. Thankfully, our zoos provide creative and meaningful opportunities for children to participate in conservation.

So what have we zoo professionals learned about giant pandas? First, we have learned how precious few of these splendid creatures are left on the earth. And we understand now that we must work long and hard to protect each and every one of them. As I see it, those few zoos having the opportunity to exhibit them have a special obligation to share the experience with others. As we learn about them, we must also disseminate the new knowledge by publication in reputable journals, making it available to other scholars worldwide. We are already making videotape available on television and on the World Wide Web so distant populations may experience the joy and wonder of the pandas.

We have learned also that it is the Chinese people who will ultimately save the giant panda from extinction. Just as certainly, however, we are destined to be their partners in this expensive and intellectually challenging endeavor. Zoos worldwide will play an important role in the struggle to save the giant panda, and limited exhibitions in big cities such as Mexico City, San Diego, Tokyo, Berlin, and Atlanta will generate the necessary goodwill and public commitment. Our most important contribution may be the relationships that we are forming with our colleagues in China. This will be a legacy of peace, cooperation, and trust that could easily have greater social ramifications beyond panda conservation. As the citizens of our two countries reach out to dialogue, debate, and understand, much can be accomplished to our mutual benefit. Pandas may indeed be ambassadors of peace and understanding. If this proposition is true, their survival takes on a new urgency and a far deeper meaning.

The giant panda is the world's most charismatic creature. Its fascinating story can provide a foundation for a lifelong interest in the world's wildlife. Our children will participate in a lifetime of dedicated protection for pandas and other creatures at risk of extinction, and this will be a far better world for their efforts.

Newt Gingrich once told me, "America is surely rich enough to save giant pandas and other endangered creatures." I believed it then, and I believe it now, but we must be spiritually rich enough to follow through on our commitment, to act decisively on their behalf. In this political year, what we do for giant pandas may put conservation back on the American agenda. If so, pandas will have proved their mettle as the Creator's most inspirational critter.

# – REFERENCES –

Ball, N. 1984. "A Panda's First Year." *Zoogoer* 13, 18–21.

Beever, E. 2000. "The Roles of Optimism in Conservation Biology." *Conservation Biology* 14, 3, 907–909.

Berkovitz, A. 1997. "China's Revolution in Education." *Wildlife Conservation*, January/February, 45–49.

Blair, W. R. 1938. "Pandora in Her New Home." *Bulletin of the New York Zoological Society* 41, 4, 119–122.

Brambell, M. R. 1976. "The Giant Panda (Ailuropoda melanoleuca)." *Transactions of the Zoological Society of London* 33, 85–92.

Campbell, J. and Qin, Z. 1983. "Interaction of Giant Pandas, Bamboo, and People." *Journal of the American Bamboo Society* 4, 1–35.

David, A. 1869. "Voyage en Chine." *Nouv. Arch. Mus. Hist. Nat. Paris* 5, 3–13.

Drew, L. 1989. "Are we loving the panda to death?" *National Wildlife* 27, 1, 14–17.

Gold, K. and Maple, T. L. 1994. "Personality Assessment in the Gorilla and Its Utility as a Management Tool." *Zoo Biology* 13, 509–522.

Harlow, H. F. 1971. *Learning to Love*. Chicago, Aldine.

Harlow, H. F. and Mears, C. 1976. *The Human Model: Primate Perspectives*. New York, Winston/Wiley.

Hediger, H. 1930. *Wild Animals in Captivity*. London, Butterworths.

Hediger, H. 1966. *Man and Animal in the Zoo*. London, Routledge, Kegan & Paul.

Johnson, K. G. 1988. "Comparative behavior of red and giant pandas in the Wolong Reserve, China." *Journal of Mammalogy* 69, 552–564.

Kleiman, D. 1978. "Five Years with Ling-Ling and Hsing-Hsing." *Zoogoer* 5, 9–11.

Kleiman, D. 1983. "Ethology and reproduction of captive giant pandas (Ailuropoda melanoleuca)." *Zeitschrift fur Tierpsychologie* 62, 1–46.

Kotler, R. & Roberto, E. L. 1989. *Social Marketing*. New York, Free Press.

Lindburg, D. G., Huang, X. M. and Huang, S. Q. "Reproductive Performance of Giant Panda Males in Chinese Zoos." In Zhang, A. and He, G. (Eds.). *Proceedings of the International Symposium on the Protection of the Giant Panda (A. Melanoleuca).* Chengdu, China, Sichuan Publishing House of Science and Technology, 67–71.

Lorenz, K. 1966. *On Aggression*. New York, Harcourt.

Lu, Z. 1999. "Update of WWF's Panda Conservation Programme." *Report to WWF China Programme*, January.

Lu, Z., Pan, W. and Harkness, J. 1994. "Mother-Cub Relationships in Giant Pandas in the Qinling Mountains, China, with Comment on Rescuing Abandoned Cubs." *Zoo Biology* 13, 6, 567–568.

Mainka, S. A. and Zhang, H. 1994. "Daily Activity of Captive Giant Pandas (Ailuropoda melanoleluca) at the Wolong Reserve." *Zoo Biology* 13, 1, 13–20.

Maple, T.L. and Hoff, M.P. 1982. *Gorilla Behavior*. New York, Van Nostrand Reinhold Co.

Maple, T. L., Perkins, L. A. and Snyder, R. 1997. "The Role of Environmental and Social Variables in the Management of Apes and Pandas." Paper delivered at the 1997 Symposium on the Conservation of the Giant Panda and Other Endangered Species.

Milne-Edwards. "Estrait d'une lettre de meme (M. l'Abbe David) datee de la principalite Thibetaine (independante) de Moupin, le 21 Mars, 1869." *Nouv. Mus. Arch. Hist. Nat. Paris* 5, 13.

Morris R. and Morris, D. 1966. *Men and Pandas*. New York, McGraw-Hill.

O'Brien, S. 1989. "The Ancestry of the Giant Panda." *Scientific American* 257, 5, 102–107.

Page, J. 1984. "The Panda's Past." *Zoogoer* 13, 9–17.

Pan, W. 1995. "New Hope for China's Pandas." *National Geographic* 187, 2, 100–115.

Rogers, B. R. 1994. *Giant Pandas*. New York, Friedman/Fairfax.

Ryder, O. 1987. "The Giant Panda is a Bear." *Zoonooz* 60, 8, 16.

Schaller, G. B. 1993. *The Last Panda*. Chicago, University of Chicago Press.

Shepherdson, D. J., Mellen, J. D. and Hutchins, M. (Eds.) 1998. *Second Nature: Environmental Enrichment for Captive Animals*. Washington, D.C., Smithsonian Institution Press.

Snyder, R. , Zhong, W., Xiangming, H. and Maple, T. L. 1997. "Breeding Season Behavior of Female and Male Giant Pandas at the Chengdu Zoo and the Chengdu Research Base of Giant Panda Breeding." Paper presented at the 1997 Chengdu Symposium on Giant Pandas and other Endangered Species.

Swaisgood R. R., White, A. M., Zhou, X., Zhang, H.,

Wei, R., Hare, V. J., Tepper, E. M. and Lindburg, D. G. (In press.) "A quantitative assessment of the efficacy of an environmental enrichment program for giant pandas." *Animal Behaviour*.

Tellez-Giron, J. A. 1980. "Giant Pandas in Chapultepec Park Zoo, Mexico City." *International Zoo Yearbook* 20, 264–269.

Wilson, S. C. and Kleiman, D. 1974. "Eliciting Play: A Comparative Study." *American Zoologist* 143, 341–370.

Wilson, R. A. 1996. "Environmental education programs for preschool children." *Journal of Environmental Education* 27, 4, 28–33.

Yerkes, R. M. 1925. *Almost Human*. New York, Century.

Zhu, X., Lindburg, D. G., Pan, W., Forney, K., and Wang, D. 2000. "The Reproductive Strategy of Giant Pandas (Ailuropoda melanoleuca): Infant Growth and Development and Mother-Infant Relationships." *Journal of Zoology*, London 252, in press.